A Hazardous Melody of Being:
Seóirse Bodley's Song Cycles
on the Poems of Micheal O'Siadhail

A Hazardous Melody of Being:
Seóirse Bodley's Song Cycles
on the Poems of Micheal O'Siadhail

An Apograph

edited by Lorraine Byrne Bodley

Carysfort Press

A Carysfort Press Book in association with Peter Lang

A Hazardous Melody of Being:

Bodley's Song Cycles on O'Siadhail's Poems

An Apograph edited by Lorraine Byrne Bodley

First published in Ireland in 2008 by Carysfort Press Ltd
58 Woodfield, Scholarstown Road, Dublin 16, Ireland
ISBN 978-1-78997-089-0

© 2008 Copyright of this edition of the music remains with the editor

Cover design by Brian O'Connor

Typeset by Carysfort Press Ltd

This book is published with the financial assistance of The Arts Council (An Chomhairle Ealaíon), Dublin, Ireland, under the Title by Title Scheme

Caution: All rights reserved. No part of this book may be printed or reproduced or utilized in any form or by any electronic, mechanical, or other means, now known or hereafter invented including photocopying and recording, or in any information storage or retrieval system without permission in writing from the publishers.

Biographies

Seóirse Bodley was born in Dublin 1933. Studies in Ireland and Germany led to an appointment in the Music Department of University College Dublin, of which he is an Emeritus Professor. Influences on his compositions include a range of musical styles from the European avant-garde to Irish traditional music. Works include five symphonies, two chamber symphonies, and numerous orchestral, choral, vocal, and chamber pieces. Commissions he has received include his Third Symphony, commissioned for the opening of the National Concert Hall in Dublin, and his Fourth Symphony, commissioned by the Arturo Toscanini Symphony Orchestra of Parma, Italy. His music has been performed and broadcast in Ireland, North America, Europe, and China. Awards include the Arts Council Prize for Composition, a Travelling Studentship of the National University of Ireland, the Macaulay Fellowship in Music Composition, and the Marten Toonder Award. He is a founder-member of *Aosdána*, Ireland's academy of eminent creative artists and President of the Association of Irish composers.

Micheal O'Siadhail's latest collection of poetry, *Globe*, was published in January 2007. Among eleven collections are *Love Life* (2005), *The Gossamer Wall: Poems in Witness to the Holocaust* (2002) and *Poems 1975-1995* (1995). Awards include: an Irish American Cultural Institute (1982) prize, a Toonder prize (1998) and short-listed for Wingate Jewish Quarterly Prize (2003).

O'Siadhail has been lecturer (Trinity College Dublin) and professor (Dublin Institute for Advanced Studies). Academic works include *Learning Irish* (Yale University Press) and *Modern Irish* (Cambridge University Press). He is a former member of Arts Council of the Republic of Ireland (1988-93), founder member of *Aosdána* (Academy of distinguished Irish artists), former editor of *Poetry Ireland Review*, founding chairman Ireland Literature Exchange.

O'Siadhail's poem suites, *The Naked Flame*, *The Earlsfort Suite* (with Seóirse Bodley), *Summerfest* (with Colman Pearce), and *Dublin Spring* (with James Wilson) were commissioned and set to music for performance and broadcasting. His work has been translated into several languages and there are books in Japanese and German: *Madamu Jazu Yookoso* (Shichigatsudoo, Tokyo 1999), *Bokutachi No NijuToki* (Shichigatsudoo, Tokyo 2001) and *Aus Heiterem Himmel* (Heiderhoff Verlag, Eisingen, 2001). A Japanese translation of *The Gossamer Wall* is due later this year.

Lorraine Byrne Bodley is a Lecturer at the Department of Music, NUI Maynooth. She holds a PhD in German and Music from University College Dublin. Awards include the Goethe Prize of the English Goethe Society (2001), a DAAD scholarship, and an IRCHSS

Government of Ireland Post-Doctoral Fellowship (2001-03). Dr Byrne Bodley has published nine books. She is the sole author of two books: *Schubert's Goethe Settings* (Ashgate, 2003) and *Goethe and Zelter: Musical Dialogues* (Ashgate, forthcoming 2008). She has edited five volumes of musicological essays and critical editions of scores: *The Unknown Schubert* (Ashgate, forthcoming 2008) co-edited with the Canadian scholar, Barbara Reul (University of Regina). She is the sole editor of *Proserpina: Monodrama by Goethe with Music by Carl Eberwein* (Carysfort Press, 2007) and *Goethe: Musical Poet, Musical Catalyst* (Carysfort Press, 2004). She is co-editor with Dan Farrelly of *Goethe and Schubert: Across the Divide* (Carysfort Press, 2003) and a piano reduction of *Claudine von Villa Goethe's Singspiel set by Franz Schubert* (Carysfort Press, 2002). This is the second apograph she has produced with Seóirse Bodley. The first, *Seóirse Bodley: Three Congregational Masses*, was published by Carysfort Press in 2005.

Editorial Note

The two scores which follow present, with very little change, the works written in 1987 and 2000. The main difference is that *The Earlsfort Suite* appears here in a version for piano rather than in full score. In this published version Bodley has made minor alterations to the original particell to render in terms of the piano the essence of his original orchestral score. Although the cycle misses out on the many colours of a modern orchestra, it gains a certain amount in the piano writing, an example of which is the very resonant sound available in the closing bars, where the piano's sustaining pedal is depressed and many strings resound simultaneously.

When editing *The Naked Flame,* the copy of the manuscript I was working from was laden with performance directions from concerts given in former years. In these additional directions Bodley breaks through conventional limitations on expression – luminous, starry dance, desolate – his aim being to render a performance of great musical intensity. It reminded me of some of the instructions used by Mahler *schreiend* (screaming) in the orchestral version of 'Der Tamboursg'sell', and in his *Kindertotenlieder*: *mit Erschütterung* (with deep distress) and *mit ausbrechendem Schmerz* (breaking out in pain) in the first and third songs respectively. For this reason, I decided to include in this apograph these directions, the most remarkable aspect of which is their great refinement. Nuance is of paramount importance to Bodley; detailed indications and subtle distinctions abound in these songs, where he calculates expression with meticulous precision. Although the composer continually explores changing dynamic colour, his dynamic signs are far from being merely precise indications of volume and weight; the same sign may be interpreted differently in different songs. In these cycles, extreme dynamics serve principally a psychological function – to emphasize the human dimension of the music – rather than the practical purpose of indicating precise degrees of loudness.

When discussing song it is important not to ignore the extra-musical analysis: to do so is to ignore the aesthetic out of which song grows. Consequently, I have sought to unveil the background to the poems and highlight their significance in their own right as well as their importance in this musical context. In discussing the songs, however, I have tended to focus on their interpretation in relation to the musical setting – an approach I feel entirely fitting to the introduction for an apograph.

Finally, in writing this apograph, I have endeavoured to make as quintessential a statement as I could of what seems an important case. What the case is, the title of the introduction, 'A Tradition Redefined: Seóirse Bodley's Song Cycles On the Poems of Micheal O'Siadhail', will, I hope, show quite plainly. The reader, I trust, will recognize that at the very heart of my discussion of these cycles is my concern for the needs and prospects of contemporary art song in a time of relative neglect in Ireland. It would be rash to maintain that the morale of Irish art song at the present hour is high or that its performers face the future with the confidence in their art enjoyed by performers of the nineteenth and early twentieth centuries. We are living in the aftermath of a great song era, to which the specifically Irish contribution was, on the whole, unremarkable. There are, of course, such fine exceptions as Frederick May's *Songs from Prison* and the solo songs of Aloys Fleischmann. Like May and Fleischmann, Bodley's and O'Siadhail's artistic traditions were cradled within that of European music and poetry as a whole, and I should like to see that wholeness restored and with it our own place in the common endeavour. The broad emphasis of my introduction, therefore, has fallen upon one aspect of art song – its relation to private and public morality in the extreme circumstances of a century which has brought immense upheaval to European civilization. Against this backdrop of cultural and social change, there is much to encourage us in what has been achieved in the writing of these song cycles. We need, in a time of change and evasion, to strike through to some certainties. The main contention of this apograph is, therefore, that song at its most responsible still has immense resources, and will not easily be deflected from pursuing and setting down indelibly its own form of truth.

Lorraine Byrne Bodley
January 2008

Acknowledgements

It is a pleasure to acknowledge the assistance and encouragement of many friends and colleagues during the planning and preparation of this apograph. From the start Seóirse was unstinting in his help and wise counsel. My introduction to this apograph greatly benefited from discussions with him about the song cycles. I have enjoyed the privilege of a private performance of these cycles in our home, where Seóirse sang and played through the works for me. The memory of this performance has informed my writing. It is a pleasure to thank particularly Micheal and Brid O'Siadhail for the hospitality shown to me and to record the warmth of their welcome when I visited them to discuss the poetry of these song cycles. I am immensely grateful to Micheal O'Siadhail for reading an early version of my introductory essay and for making many valuable suggestions. To Professor David Ford, Regis Professor of Divinity at the University of Cambridge, and Dr Marc Caball, Director of the University College Dublin Humanities Institute of Ireland, both of whom wrote letters of recommendation for this book, I owe my warm thanks. I am most grateful to the National University of Ireland, Maynooth, to the National University of Ireland, and to the Arts Council, all of whom have generously supported this book.

In preparing this apograph for publication, I am greatly indebted to Dr Dan Farrelly, General Editor of Carysfort Press, whose sensitivity and judgement I have always valued very highly indeed. Not only did he read my introductory essay carefully, he has also been a source of support for many years, first as an inspiring teacher, later, as a valued colleague, and always as a friend. I am grateful to the talented Brian O'Connor for his attractive cover designs for all my books with Carysfort Press. My thanks are due to Succession H. Matisse Paris who graciously granted permission to publish Matisse, *Icarus* (*Jazz*) as our cover image; I am also indebted to Nicole Rivette, Associate Registrar for Collections Rights & Permissions at the Toledo Museum of Art, Ohio, for the electronic image of that print. The title of this montage shares a coincidental link with the student literary publication, *Icarus*, founded by Alec Reid, an English lecturer at Trinity in 1950. The success of this journal in the 1960s was indicative of the cultural energy of Trinity during this period when O'Siadhail was a student. And it is interesting that an early poem by O'Siadhail published in *Icarus*[1] should make reference to the snows of 1947 which reappear here in *Earlsfort Suite*.

The pleasure of writing is always increased by those dear friends with whom we first share our ideas. My thanks to Professor Harry White, Professor of Music at University College Dublin, for his immediate understanding when I first mentioned this book to him: I owe him much. It is a pleasure to remember Dr Gareth Cox – whose company I have

---

[1] 'Born just before the snow began...', *Icarus* (1967), ed. Nicholas Grene.

enjoyed on his many visits to our home during his own scholarly engagement with Seóirse's music – and my colleagues at Maynooth for their unfailing good faith and friendship.

This book, written in celebration of Seóirse Bodley's seventy-fifth year, will be launched at a concert of both cycles performed by Sylvia O'Brien (soprano) and Seóirse Bodley (piano) in the Hugh Lane Gallery, Dublin, on 20 April 2008. I am greatly indebted to the organizer of the Sundays at Noon concerts at the Hugh Lane Gallery, Gavin O'Sullivan, who cheerfully responded to an array of questions concerning the performance of these cycles. My warm thanks to Professor Hormoz Farhat, who readily agreed to launch the book, and to Sylvia O'Brien, whose professionalism and fine voice I have always greatly admired.

Three other singers must be mentioned: Bernadette Greevy, whose excellent performances of both of these cycles I vividly remember and to whom *The Naked Flame* is dedicated; Aylish Kerrigan, who has done much to promote Seóirse's music over the years; and my own vivacious daughter, Bláthnaid, who longs to be a diva like these fine women. Finally, I extend my warm thanks to Jane Keune Carty: it is to her own musicality and love of the art that we owe the commissioning of *The Naked Flame* during her time in RTÉ. Over the years she has always been interested in Seóirse's music; I am more sorry than I can say that her husband, Wil, did not live to enjoy this celebration.

Lorraine Byrne Bodley

A Tradition Redefined: Seóirse Bodley's Song Cycles on the Poems of Micheal O'Siadhail

Bodley and O'Siadhail: An Artistic Encounter

The encounter in the early 1980s between the composer Seóirse Bodley and the poet Micheal O'Siadhail occurred at a time when the first revolts against artistic modernism had just manifested themselves. Independently of this direction, both Bodley and O'Siadhail had separately concluded that the compositional methods they had relied on in the past did not satisfy the development of their artistic ideas. Bodley had already critically appraised the direction contemporary art was taking which led to his breaking with the avant-garde. O'Siadhail had effected the transition from collections of individual poems to books of sequences and overall thematic concerns. Their mutual contact not only had considerable consequences for the further development of the two artists themselves but also had profound implications for the evolution of Irish art song in general.

We are currently entering the seventy-fifth year since Seóirse Bodley's birth, the public celebration of which will be marked by a performance of his settings of O'Siadhail's poetry, performed by the composer with soprano, Sylvia O'Brien. In 2007 Bodley composed 'Squall' to mark the Trinity celebrations of O'Siadhail's sixtieth year. Such gestures are the artistic hallmarks of a firm friendship rooted in shared interests and shared perceptions. Both artists can encounter Irish poetry and mythology in its own language, which enables a unique identification with an Ireland outside central European tradition. Despite being attentively rooted in national tradition, both artists are adventurously cosmopolitan in outlook and have reached beyond Ireland to imagine and define their artistic practice. O'Siadhail has been greatly influenced by other European traditions from the Scandanavian to German and French, but also in later years, Japanese. Bodley has been greatly interested in the achievements of European musicians, from Stockhausen's *Gruppen für drei Orchester* and *Gesang der Jünglinge* to Boulez's *Pli selon pli*; from Berio's *Circles* and *Sinfonia* to Grisey's *Quatre Chants pour franchir le seuil*; from Schoenberg's *Das Buch der hängenden Gärten* (1908/9) to the songs of Hanns Eisler and Charles Ives. The hold these traditions have for Bodley and O'Siadhail springs from a desire to establish human identity out of the tensions and debates about national traditions and questions of identity. Both artists are formalist or experimental as the mood takes them, and they offer in their variousness compelling examples of the range and scope of Irish art song (written with confidence for an increasingly international audience) as it enters the twenty-first century. These song cycles attest to the power and image of Irish music and poetry in the world and they reflect some of the questions that have made contemporary Irish art song so interesting: the question of whether there is a monolithic tradition of Irish song or at least a dual tradition – one trying to build on a fractured musical past or one that invents its own language.

The Witness of Poetry
In his lecture on 'The Social Function of Poetry', T.S. Eliot claimed that poetry performed a social function in the 'largest sense', because it could 'affect the speech and sensibility of the whole nation'.[1] For Eliot the condition of poetry is at once the support and index of a civilization. Through O'Siadhail this tradition of public responsibility, long established in Irish poetry, is brought to new focus. In the foreword to *Poems 1975-1995* O'Siadhail acknowledges his debt to such diverse poets as Hopkins, Frost, Auden and Kavanagh; Early Irish nature poetry; Irish folk love poetry; the Scandanavian tradition; the classical poets Homer, Catullus, and Virgil; and to the symbolist tradition from Paul Valéry to Rilke.[2] O'Siadhail's list explains his poetic identity in terms of internationalism, claiming a natural complicity in several cultures: Irish, English, French, German, American, Norwegian, Swedish, and the possession of world consciousness as well as local allegiances. O'Siadhail's peregrine imagination acknowledges not only a heritage but more importantly the idea that the poet is one of a fraternity, which determines his standing and also enables him to assume it. In assuming this responsibility, O'Siadhail demands of poetry what it can offer in a postmodern age. The poems of these cycles take the form of a lyrical diary, a record of privileged moments, worked into sequence; their triumph is found in the extension of the lyrical mode, through being constantly aware of private experience in the light of history.

Theodor Adorno believed that the horror of Auschwitz made poetry impossible to write – an opinion which is often quoted.[3] When lives are annihilated in their thousands, and all sense of identity is wiped out, what can poetry do but fall silent? In such devastated areas of recent history where language rings hollow, what voices are still audible when you reap the whirlwind? For O'Siadhail the poet has no right of immunity: in *The Gossamer Wall* he commemorates those forgotten who perished through the inhuman cataclysm and terrors of Nazi genocide. His poems of witness haunt new margins of mortality and literary memorial as he contemplates the ruins of a Europe he has adopted as his own. The assumption of such poetic responsibility was acknowledged by Ezra Pound in his essay, 'The Serious Artist', where he explains the essence of poetry as 'art that bears true witness'.[4] While it has always been the function of poetry at its best to describe, to put on record, what the many feel but cannot understand or articulate, the experience of Irish poets over the last century has made this a compelling need. It has called for 'the art that is most precise' wanted by Pound and a fullness of response that are nothing new in Irish literary history. Bodley's generation, which grew up in the 1930s and 1940s, was plunged into a divided and perplexed era that has continued to this day. For half a century now we have witnessed the breaking of human lives, of established continuities, and its artists have borne a heavy responsibility. In such times O'Siadhail has kept true to conscience, and his capacity to respond to the unexpected gives the poet his assurance. Like Heaney, Mahon and Muldoon the poetic experience he records is deeply engaged with the complexities of the age we inhabit. In contrast to many Northern poets, O'Siadhail's witness has recovered for our time much of its religious meaning: he testifies to the truth and in a century of false testimony he becomes a witness to man. In tracing O'Siadhail's heritage one is reminded of the trochees of Auden's elegy:

> Follow, poet, follow right
> To the bottom of the night,
> With your unconstraining voice
> Still persuade us to rejoice

which stress the poet's aspiration to inspire individual and universal human dignity. Such responsibility towards the human condition is intensely and commendably strong in the meditative poems of *The Naked Flame*.

Song and the Shape of History

Does song play a new role in twentieth-century music or was this the age, as many have insisted, that bears witness to the 'death of song'? The old imbroglio, 'What are the salient features of twentieth-century song?', is difficult to answer not because of lack of historical evidence but because of the tendency to chart historicist trajectories for nineteenth- and twentieth-century song. Ultimately, how one answers such questions depends on how one views contemporary song. I incline to a socially informed meaning, where the discourse on culture is not confined to literary circles. Herder conceived song as the true voice of the people;[5] Nietzsche called it 'the musical mirror of the world ... the original melody'.[6] No less than in bygone centuries, contemporary song inscribes individual concerns and mirrors the influence of dominant social trends through its music and its texts. Beyond such musico-poetic analysis, a reading of the threefold roles of continuity, gradual change, and revolution together opens up a 'braided history' of Irish art song, where song is not an aesthetic given but a means to understanding the changing patterns of life. An understanding of the way in which Irish society has perceived song in recent centuries is available through a consideration of song as social document, bearing witness to different ways in which song has been located in our cultural history. Although such a trajectory lies beyond the scope of this essay, it is important, nonetheless, when appraising Bodley's O'Siadhail settings, to consider the importance of these songs as a reflection of our cultural history. Today, with art song of minor importance in modern concert life, one tends to overlook its significance.

Reconfiguring Irish Art Song

Seóirse Bodley engaged with art song for many reasons, even for radical experiment. This one small genre supplies an abundant yield, especially with regard to the composer's eclectic style. In contrast to many twentieth-century composers, Bodley shows individuality in his attitude towards song, which unequivocally occupies a central position and has important significance in other areas of Bodley's creativity. Within song's intimate setting, Bodley was able to convey musical thoughts and gestures unavailable in his larger works. His settings of Irish poets were a compositional testing ground and in his writing of Irish art song one finds profound and finely wrought expression.

Bodley's break with the tradition of art song in Ireland is no simple step into a new world of sound. For years the composer had sought new paths in music, poetry, and painting. Yeats, Kavanagh, McGreevy, Kennelly, and O'Siadhail all entered an inner realm that fascinated Bodley; so too had the painters, Paul Klee, Mondrian, and Matisse. To convert such artistic expression into music, Bodley was continually in search of new modes of lyrical expression, new ways of blurring tonal feeling. In his song cycles to the poems of Kennelly and O'Siadhail, Bodley had a double aesthetic aim or a 'dialectical aesthetic'[7]: he wanted to advance Irish song into modernity and to preserve an inherited European tradition. With each poet, he approached this objective in different ways.

Bodley's O'Siadhail settings bear witness to a melding of innovation and tradition, the nurturing ground from which his radical ideas spring. His settings express his aim for a modern lyricism, careful musical organization and, above all, evocative mood – aspects of traditional song which he sought to preserve in a modern context. Bodley's O'Siadhail settings are examples of free configurations, where the musical form seems to depend almost entirely on the poetry for coherence. Such dominance of poetry can be traced to the early aesthetics of German art song in the so-called *Goethezeit*, where the term 'Lied' oscillated between poetical and musical components. The songs in question here can also be placed within the tradition of the German song cycle. Indeed *The Naked Flame* is very much a song cycle, but not in the tradition of a *Liederkreis* defined by Beethoven and early Schubert, with a clear narrative structure as found in Bodley's Kennelly cycle, *A Girl*. Instead, Bodley's O'Siadhail settings follow the trajectory of the *Liederreihe*, a cycle without a narrative, using traditional musical means by which the composer endeavours to achieve cyclic unity. A few examples regarding three major parameters may suffice:

(a) Thematic references at key moments, points of attraction, the beginning and the end in particular, are one element. 'Tuning In' (no.1) and 'Rhapsody' (no.12) share musical ideas, stressing the related philosophic content of the poems. The rondo theme in no. 2 is paralleled by a related recurring theme in O'Siadhail's companion poem, 'Initiation'. The discovery of desire in 'Debonair' (no.5) and 'Hovering' (no. 12) is mirrored in the direct inter-relationship of the two accompaniments.

(b) Identical rhythmic patterns related to a melodic cell and forming a quasi-motif are another unifying means. A good example of this in the *Earlsfort Suite* is the unifying significance of melodic passages based on chords of superimposed thirds.

(c) A harmonic connection or 'chords' built upon 12 notes (11 pitches), is obvious in many pieces of *The Naked Flame*. It is presented in the opening bars of the cycle and is freely used throughout the cycle, with its strictest realizations in 'Tuning In' (no.1), bars 1 and 91 where most of the 12 notes are left vibrating, and 'A Closure' (no.9), bar 1 to bars 555-56 where the opening statement is recalled for the musical climax of the cycle.

(d) In addition, Bodley composed direct connections between several songs as Schumann did in *Dichterliebe* (nos.1 through 3, for example). In *The Naked Flame* Bodley makes directions from bar 1 (no.1) to bar 179 (no.2); bar 1 to bars 412 (no.6) and 591 (no.9) where the two chords of bar 1 switch hands; bar 1 to bars 473-73, 476-78 and 480-85 where the second chord appears in a triplet figuration.

(e) Bodley also wrote instrumental connections between several of the songs, including cross-references that function as musical commentaries. Bodley's postlude to the portrayal of a young girl in 'Debonair' (no.5), for example, recurs in 'Hovering' (no.11), the musical portrait of matured desire, thereby providing subtle instrumental commentary. The opening of the cycle is rendered with slight variation in the closing bars of 'Return' (no.7) and 'Rhapsody' (no.12). In 'Initiation' (no.11) Bodley picks up on the poetic chiasma and refers back to 'Rondo for Eamonn' (no.2) this time using a recurring pentatonic tune rather than a rondo theme.

(f) Certainly the instrumentation has its function for cyclic ordering in the *Earlsfort Suite*. The central piece, 'Rite of Passage', uses instrumentation which accentuates the fragmentation of the music creating a mood of anticipation and nervousness. The vibraphone appears only in the middle movement adding its own nervous vibration to the held notes played with bowed tremolos by the middle strings (bar 64ff.) The finale has the 'heaviest load': all instruments participate in the opening and the postlude. At the same time the finale shares with the opening movement a careful attention to orchestration which allows the voice to remain prominent.

(g) Certain songs are designed for their specific place and function in *The Naked Flame*. No.12 is written as a finale; the beginning of no.1 has an introductory gesture; nos.2 and 10 are clearly companion pieces to mirror the chiasma in O'Siadhail's cycle; 'A Closure' is the dramatic climax of the work.

Lyricism and Modernity

Bodley's O'Siadhail cycles form a Janus-faced genre simultaneously advancing the spirit of innovation and preserving an inherited tradition. Bodley responds to art song, a lyrical genre, and at the same time seeks unconventional ways to emphasize words: one way is through long 'florid' melismas of descriptive intent as in 'Hekla's fire' (*Earlsfort Suite*, 'Delivery', bars 19-22) and 'As lava of pure desire comes scrolling down' ('Delivery', bars 49-53). Another is by setting emotive words to longer time values, as if to extract musically the utmost feeling the words can convey. See, for example, his setting of the words 'months' and 'Fates' in 'Rite of Passage' (*Earlsfort Suite*, bars 79 and 114). The third, most forceful, means is through the use of wide leaps, an important part of Bodley's expressive style. They serve to galvanize the melody, to give an image to words of direction: 'Your road out, my road back' (*The Naked Flame*, 'Initiation', bars 671-75); or even to heighten intense emotion: 'I grieve for you' and 'I'll search for you' (*The Naked Flame*, 'A Closure', bars 591-92 and 596).[8] The lyrical impulse and free-ranging tonality of these songs confirm Bodley's stylistic estrangement from the avant-garde composers of the Darmstadt school. In comparison to contemporary European songs, these settings exhibit considerable harmonic support in their underpinning,[9] yet many of the songs present challenges for even the professional performer. They are refined songs, which greatly enrich our concert repertory.

The Naked Flame

The Naked Flame locates itself on the threshold of past and present, wisdom and innocence, selfhood and community, poetry and truth. In this cycle O'Siadhail does not disguise from himself life's tragic contradictions – an attitude that underscores the poet's celebration of life and gives the key to understanding the complexity of the world. This ideal balance between seriousness and play, tragic awareness and delight in living, brings to mind the well-known declaration of Yeats: 'We begin to live when we have conceived life as tragedy.'[10] Between Yeats and O'Siadhail there are both affinities and opposition. While Yeats's creation of a 'special Anglo-Irish culture' has faded in O'Siadhail's poetry before the Joycean impulse for immersion in the modern tide of global modernity, both are poets who have evolved towards what Yeats called 'responsibilities'.[11] Eliot has described Yeats in terms which apply no less to O'Siadhail. Eliot admired Yeats for 'an exceptional honesty and courage' in facing the need for 'adaptation to the years'.[12] Poetry requires the courage, in Keats's words, to endure 'being in uncertainties, mysteries, doubts'.[13] Nineteenth-century optimism, twentieth-century despair – not that either attitude was total at any time – are alike in their unwillingness to face that suspension between extremes and to live undaunted by contradiction. Most admirable of all in O'Siadhail is his ability to accept the sense of the ambiguous and irresolvable in human life, and to use this sense, with all its discomfort, as the material for his poetry.

Although most poetry in modern times is meant to be spoken, some poetry is meant to be sung; this cycle of poems began its musical life in RTÉ's commission of Seóirse Bodley to write a second song cycle.[14] Having composed a song cycle with a tightly-woven narrative in Brendan Kennelly's *A Girl*, Bodley now sought a cycle which would move away from the conventional song cycle towards a more abstract song row. O'Siadhail's answer was to write two meditative poems, the first, 'Tuning In' (no.1) forming an entrance to the cycle, the second, 'Rhapsody' (no.12) providing closure: between these two doorways are ten poems which explore life's essence, 'the naked flame'. The inner songs of the cycle are characterized more as individual pieces in a variety of moods framed by two meditative pieces more pointed towards philosophical truths.[15]. The central theme of the cycle is the vulnerability of the human condition, particularly as viewed from the middle years, where one no longer looks only forward but also back to one's youth. In a note on the text, O'Siadhail unveils how 'the poems focus on our human vulnerability to the joys and falls of living; by laying ourselves open to life's flame we grow and deepen'.[16] This idea is explored in different ways through the pattern of inner poems, lending unity to the varied scenes of O'Siadhail's cycle. 'The overall sequence of the poems suggests a life-cycle with patterns of change and recurrence, healing and renewal'.[17] A central question in considering this musical cycle is how Bodley shifts attention from the sides – the opening and closing songs – to the main body of settings. Bodley, no less than O'Siadhail, was eminently aware that the mysteries of existence are revealed in privileged moments. In the middle settings he softens contrast, yet deepens its implications through subtle craft and assigns to contrast the role of expressing a poem's unstated, implied or symbolic connotations. This thread taken up from the opening poem is subtly woven through the middle movements or character pieces. As individual lyrical movements these inner character pieces can represent different states of a subjective mind; ordered sequences of such scenes forming a process, designed and directed by a modern lyrical 'plot'. Yet how do we understand this hidden plot of *The Naked Flame*, especially the open ending, and in particular, what is the role of music in conveying its meaning?

T.S. Eliot declared, 'In my beginning is my end.'[18] Bodley conceives O'Siadhail's cycle in such a way: the whole thing is based on twelve notes in the final bar (bar 816) which is not a formal twelve-note row since the G is doubled.

Example 1: Bodley, *The Naked Flame*, 'Rhapsody', piano, bar 186

The opening chord of the piece is the upper six notes and the second chord is the lower six notes. Here Bodley is seeking new ways to unify the cycle, to find a substitute for the musical order that tonality imparts. By recalling the initial bars in the postlude, Bodley conveys a sense of structural balance in this cycle. Within the body of the cycle he reconfigures the 'chords', reshaping them asymmetrically or altering their textures freely. Musical symbolism plays an important part in his tonal aesthetics: the higher six notes are associated with the future, the lower six notes represent the past. Throughout *The Naked Flame* various appearances of the twelve-note chord underscore recurring ideas of impermanence, the balance of opposites, hovering, hurt, and living in the moment. Bodley's use of tonal symbolism provides this work with its broad structure, its 'organizing frame'. The first and final movements frame the cycle because they function as mainstays or buttresses, enclosing the inner songs. The finale serves also as a denouement for the work's tonal symbolism. By presenting motivic puzzles in the opening movements that he resolves in the finale, Bodley ties the poetic symbolism to the musical structure. Through this approach he explores new paths by revitalizing older concepts of song; he is the first Irish composer to meet this challenge in song in this manner.

Although the entire work is largely generated from these two sets of notes, the songs of *The Naked Flame* show great variety. Bodley sought to capture its lyricism, its rich colours, and the cycle's inner world. He floods the piano part with colour, tone painting, characterization, realism and naturalism. The cycle embodies many styles of song: lyrical songs with a gentle evocative mood ('A Toast on the Eve'); dramatic song ('A Closure'); and declamatory song ('Rondo for Eamonn' (bars 108-09; 118-19; 162-63); the recitative ending of 'Those we follow' (bars 293-98); and 'Hurt' (bars 389, 391 and 394). While this ripe harvest reflects the work of a serious composer, the variety of songs makes it a demanding cycle to sing. The opening and closing songs are settings of complex philosophic verse which are interpreted in Bodley's vocal line through the protean melodic or rhythmic motives of 'Rhapsody' through to the theatrical declamation of 'Tuning In'. Within this frame Bodley explores three basic vocal styles – lyrical, dramatic, and speech-like – his modern lyrical arioso shading into each of the three. All three appear in a single setting in 'Love-song' where Bodley's dramatic style ranges from the straightforwardly declamatory through a kind of *recitativo* to the lyrical arioso. He experiments with these three styles in a single setting, 'Hurt', seeking always to fuse text and music intimately.

Throughout *The Naked Flame* Bodley uses two types of tone painting: imitation and association. The soaring dramatic writing that characterizes the composer's style is most evident in 'A Closure', in direct contrast to 'Hurt' where the vocal lines are jagged – which is characteristic of the poetic mood. Imitations in the piano are equally deft. In 'Those we follow' (no.3) an accompanying figuration moves continuously to the final line of the poem, almost as if the singer were on a journey only to be halted by the mysterious line at the end of the poem.[19] 'A Toast on the Eve' is accompanied by an unconventional twinkling star figuration which falls a step on every appearance. Most associations occur through the connotations of words. Bodley's procedure in the *Earlsfort Suite* is a familiar one used by Italian madrigalists – to relate the visualized with musical motion: the undulating movement of 'Hekla's fire' (*Earlsfort Suite*, 'Delivery', bars 19-22) is associated with the undulating vocal melody, where the rising triplets resemble the flame's rising contour. In *The Naked Flame*, words connoting motion are often set in wide leaps that bring them into sharp relief: (Watch those eyes' and 'I drown in his glance' in 'Hovering', bars 678-79 and 684-85); the expressive melodic movement of 'Debonair' (first introduced at bars 358-59); or 'Hurt' (bar 408); 'But no (I won't mourn)' which reaches E flat, the highest note in the song so far in 'A Closure'; and the deliberate pointing of the word 'love' in 'Rhapsody'. Although such musical patterns recur, each song has its own musical colour. Rhythmically some voice parts are so fluid that they seem to obscure the metre of their poetry. Yet the expressive style developed by Bodley in the finely wrought declamation of 'Return' develops the poetic, the expressive in music. Through this 'prose style' Bodley elevates Irish art song to new heights. These song texts are deeply expressive and the voice of a poet who 'has created his own tradition, is unlike any or all of the assembled troops of his predecessors'[20] gives these songs an individual stamp among Irish art songs.

'Tuning In'

For Schopenhauer, music 'represents the metaphysical of everything that is physical in the world, the thing-in-itself of every phenomenon ... Music gives at once heightened significance to every painting, indeed, to every scene of real life and of the world. It certainly does this, the more analogous the melody is to the inner spirit of a given phenomenon. This is the reason why one can set a poem to music as a song.'[21] In these cycles Bodley exploits music's supreme expressiveness in a variety of ways. The opening and closing songs of *The Naked Flame* are examples of how he gives heightened significance to O'Siadhail's philosophic description without resorting to naturalistic description. For Goethe, 'the great and noble privilege of music is to express through mood the inner core [of things] without the use of crude external means'.[22] Evident in this cycle is Bodley's synthetic approach, namely the creation of a parallel mood for the poem as a whole as well as a subtle response to textual nuances. In the opening song he invokes a feeling of insecurity by veiling the tonality through the opening chords. He heightens this feeling of uncertainty with a temporary suspension of tonality until bar 22 where it settles for the first time.

O'Siadhail's revelatory line, 'Nothing will stand still', is a counterbalance to the philosophical concept of *nunc stans*, eternity as a fixed present. The central concept of

O'Siadhail's cycle is life as ever-evolving renewal. For O'Siadhail, this flux is rife with hidden meaning: recognition of the continual movement in life alongside a recognition of a reality which is grounded in particular human lives. The *Naked Flame* suggests a wider context along with an inner reality which we experience but only in part. Bodley underscores this crucial symbol of flux with a most pregnant musical idea, an opening call to attention which he states at the beginning of the song.

Example 2: Bodley, *The Naked Flame*, 'Tuning in', piano, bars 1-2

Bodley's tightly-knit chordal structure sets up expressive musical unity in the cycle, where the basic motive serves to image the flux of life. He remoulds this idea in the piano and vocal lines each time this idea of flux is suggested.

For Bodley the mystical essence of *The Naked Flame* is focused in the opening lines of the poem. These lines reveal the significance of our fate. It permeates the melody, a long undulating line expanded from melodic fragments reflecting the rhythm of the words. It enters each strand of the linear piano part, where a veiled and quickly shifting tonality mirrors the poem's contour and heightens its mystery. Bodley links puzzles of his own to those of O'Siadhail as he merges past and future in one musical idea. The chromatic shifting through rising first inversion chords emphasizes O'Siadhail's existential dialectic: caught between something past, looking to the future, first settling at 'eternities to come' (bar 22), though significantly not on a full F sharp major chord. Being between things past and things hidden in the future is a balance which is always in motion. And as O'Siadhail's phenomenological sequence swiftly begins, the admonition, 'Look!' in the voice part, draws us into a sequence that is graphically illustrated in the piano (bars 24, 29-30). The poetic admonition to look beyond, to see how in life one thing is always hiding something else in it, is beautifully illustrated in the unfolding image of 'the lush sumac'. This song is rich in dynamic refinement and here Bodley's lush chording drifts like scents on the air. The hazy tritone with a superimposed perfect fourth in the left hand at bar 37 which stands out from Bodley's more familiar chromatic context, picks up on O'Siadhail's subtle phenomenological change to 'fragrances', signalled by the first left hand chord of the piece. Bodley's rising first inversion chords, a musical motif of past and present, form an underlay to the vocal reminder of 'bygones and tomorrow'. 'Nothing stands still' in life or in music: this musical motif is here married to the free sequence of bars 25-28 and later shared between hands in bar 64.

Bodley colours 'Tuning in' with enigmatic harmony which lends symbolic mystery to O'Siadhail's opening philosophical poem. The musical imagery of 'the lush sumac' is suitably rich and evocative, yet the changes in Siadhail's phenomenological sequence, signalled by Bodley's move towards parlando singing (bars 48-49), touches on life's hidden core – the mysteries of existence rather than on life's periphery, the sphere of naturalism. Bodley responds to O'Siadhail's symbolic imagery with musical luminescence: pentatonic scales, stark dissonance as well as gliding parallel 6/3 chords. The stark dissonance between C sharp and C natural which illuminates 'in the crow's foot' and O'Siadhail's pointed question, 'Have you so outgrown the age of time' is an 'aftertaste' of the dissonance at bar 16. The rising pentatonic scale at 'Scorch of wisdom's love or lure of madness?' ascends with a *stringendo* to a high 'D' in the vocal line. The static chording of bars 67 to 73 serves to image how we are always caught between present and past. At the clinching musical image, 'You strike the moment's note,' Bodley returns to a pentatonic scale, this time only rising to B flat at 'infinitude' yet its pressure at this musical climax is increased. The song ends with a striking musical effect, a rapid ascent (both pitch and dynamics) in the left hand where most of the twelve notes of the chromatic scale are left spinning in searching uncertainty. 'Listen to the silence' is deliberately left hanging; a musical mirror of existential uncertainties.

'Rondo For Eamonn'
Poetry hopes most of all for knowledge of life and inclines away from the perplexed, to the alternative: to be perplexed and exultant. To put it another way, O'Siadhail prefers life to be concentrated into something rich rather than something strange, a preference which is understandable if we consider poetry's constant impulse to be all truth. What is happening in 'Rondo for Eamonn' is what T.S. Eliot called 'concentration', a term which he employed when addressing the ever-pressing question of the relation between emotions actually experienced by the poet and the emotions which get expressed – or invented – in a poem. We are in the presence of such concentration when we read a poem like 'Rondo for Eamonn', where experiences of the poet's life are transferred and transformed.

The signal for Bodley's rondo theme is cued by the poetic title. The rondo symbolizes life's eternal renewal, the mystic essence of the cycle. The child's fate, revealed in this song, is not simply to grow older but to be part of life's process of eternal renewal, and the rondo theme symbolizes this eternity. In this song the balance between poet and child captures the innocence and circumscribed knowledge of a child who has not yet given in to life's uncertainty. This coming together of extremes, poet and child, in part explains why O'Siadhail's poem juxtaposes the presumably prosaic and the profound. Bodley's music contains parallel polarities, given that he conjoins the Lied's archetypal lyricism with free-ranging tonality. Throughout the song, the rondo episodes recur regularly, yet at continuously changing irregular pitch levels, a move that gives them a dual sense of reassuring predictability and unsettling randomness as in O'Siadhail's text. When the boy asks the poet questions about a painter he knew, 'Had he a studio?' the rondo anticipates the poet's recognition of life's patterns and changing roles as he recalls being twelve and talking to an artist while he prepared his canvas. The child's second question, 'Where was his studio?', a musical echo of 'Had he a studio?', is voiced a tone higher. The poignancy of the scene, heightened by the rising pitch of the questions, is musically signalled by the rondo, dovetailed by the early entry of a poet conscious of artistic lineage. Bodley underscores the poet's awareness that his response 'may float a seed in the wind' with music floating in steps in both directions; 'a seed in the wind' announced over two superimposed perfect fifths. The poet's recollections from the past are heightened by the appearance of the second chord of the piece, the composer's musical symbol of the past, which is held as the poet begins to speak. Bodley's musical reference to the opening chords mirrors O'Siadhail's awareness of past and present in 'Tuning in'. Here, as the poet looks back, the child looks forwards; Bodley mirrors this musically: 'is this the thrill of lineage' being a subtle variant of 'You know that painter you knew'; 'those agonies in the garden' accompanied by the same call to attention at the *poco meno mosso* passage in bar 141: '"O no!", he said, "My father disapproved..."' Here 'Rondo for Eamonn' – continually graced with touches of simple humanity – unveils a humble self-knowledge as the poet acknowledges the consciousness of doubt on the boy's face. Their unspoken recognition of the passing shadow on the child's face is musically signalled by three recurrences of the rondo theme, the first two in bars 202 and 208, now varied with a free flowing expressive melody above this. In the postlude it recurs without the final flourish one would expect in a classical rondo, for the story remains unfinished.

Character delineation is obviously important for the singer who wishes to transform this setting into a miniature dramatic scene. The challenge to the singer is how to delineate the three characters of this scene with contrasting vocal shades, one for each singer. Bodley characteristically helps the singer by contouring some lines after the inflections and accents of speech. His careful declamation is evident in the voicing of questions: 'dreamily a question' is musically expressed by stasis in the vocal line and a deliberate diminuendo. This naturalism is also evident in 'Had he a studio?' rendered almost entirely on the same pitch, to produce in the vocal line the idea of a question asked rather dreamily by a young boy. The poet repeats the mood of the question in a different register: 'I too am twelve.' This unity between poet and boy is musically echoed between poet and artist, where the chording at 'I watch gauche with enquiry' (bar 141) anticipates the artist's reply, 'O no!, he said.' Bodley heightens this illusion of reality in the song through contrasts of parlando passages and a lyrical line. The dramatic effect of 'A quaver in the tone triggers my subconscious' is achieved by purely musical means, through a contrasting line deliberately tending towards speech (but not intended as speech) over a programmatic descent in the bass. The implied speech rhythms of 'lightly the talk changes course' and 'I pretend not to notice the first tremble of manhood in your voice' are further examples of how Bodley interweaves dramatic elements and lyrical lines into the narrative. In 'Rondo for Eamonn' he distinguishes lyric narrative from interior monologue as sharply in music as O'Siadhail does in the poem. The composer's modern lyricism, with its intimacy and ardour of feeling, is an ideal counterpart to the poet's vernacular dialogue. The task of finding a musical parallel for interior monologue is more formidable: Bodley's answer lies in his ability to narrate musically: interest is heightened within these musical soliloquies.

'Those We Follow'
One of the most revealing questions you can ask any poet has to do with his sense of responsibility. To whom or what does he hold himself responsible in his writing? What readers – real or imaginary –, what values or principles have the right to hold him to account? When asked this question O'Siadhail replied:

> I think of Patrick Kavanagh, who, maintaining that Thomas Carlyle was too ambitious when he reckoned on a dozen readers, thought of a half dozen. I think I come down on Kavanagh's side here. There are six or seven faces who watch as I work. At the same time I trust these faces stand for humanity. As for values, I find myself wanting to speak again of a ministry of meaning, to help to find a context for our ordinary lives, to tell what rings true and maybe even to serve as a soundboard for a generation.[23]

O'Siadhail's 'six or seven faces' to which he feels answerable move beyond the type of concrete audience which constricts the imagination. Instead there is liberation in feeling responsible to this group – a representation of 'humanity' – speaking truthfully, bearing witness, offering sympathy. Ultimately the poem presents the paradox of influence: those who do not try to influence you too much have the most influence.

Bodley picks up on the literary links woven between 'Rondo for Eamonn' and 'Those we follow' and again sets the scene with a second recurrent theme. After the poet's recognition of those who 'signal praise' Bodley's fixed 2-bar figure is repeated: the left hand retains the rhythm as the treble motif rises from F to C sharp (bars 228-29) and G to D (bar 232-33). Over this the melodic content is changed as the voice tells his story of losing his way. Again Bodley's development of the poetic, the expressive in music is evident in the 'glances of light' illustrated by the high left hand chords in bars 239 and 241, in the parlando writing of 'stumbled into byways', and in the pianistic response to 'followed false signs' where the whole motif moves down into the lower register for the second stanza. The second strophe is voiced over a new harmonic resource of F sharp major granting musical assurance of the 'double loss of faith before gain'. Athough Bodley plays freely with O'Siadhail's stanzas, he imparts a sense of structural balance in the song by recalling the repeated figuration, whose accents on the final quaver render a different emphasis. He modifies this quasi-ostinato in the final stanza, altering its texture and harmony freely. His objective is for a continuity of movement and contrast, as he develops ideas from the previous stanzas to make a contrasting final stanza. Although the song seems to have divergent music for its final stanza, the composer has, instead, created contrast with similar music and in so doing, integrated text and music intimately. O'Siadhail elaborates on the nature of influence in the final stanza of this poem. Bodley does likewise, underscoring the crux of the poem with a musical reference to being caught between past and present: the recurring C natural and C flat from the opening song. The voice closes with a recitative, 'Steady as you go, you carry someone's beacon' – a reminder of living presences.

'A Toast on the Eve'

The mysterious 'A Toast on the Eve', delicate and pointillistic, provides a fine example of Bodley's light accompanying motifs. The song sparkles with a figuration prominently featuring icy perfect fourths which tinkle triple *piano* in the upper registers of the accompaniment – a direct reflection of the opening literary idea, 'Where is the star that winks in the east?' O'Siadhail's Christmas carol celebrating renewal is set against a background of uncertainty. The light ironical tone of Bodley's setting is generated by the free repetition of this recurring idea which descends a step on each appearance from C sharp (bar 299) to B (bar 313) to A (bar 326) to G (bar 337). Bodley's use of irony as an aesthetic principle is evident in his compositional perspective. In this song he uses the historicity of a common musical idiom, a twinkling star motif, as a central compositional means of realizing a distant ironic tone. Irony as a compositional principle means distancing the song from its own musical material. This enables the song to be a commentary in and on itself. Schoenberg's and Webern's very fundamental theoretical distinction between 'laws of the material' and 'laws of presentation or representation' is crucial in this respect. The compositional principle of Bodley's 'A Toast on the Eve' is not grounded in the 'laws of the material' used in this work but follow the 'laws of presentation'. The musical material, the falling star motif, is used for the presentation of an idea almost in a Brechtian sense, namely the contemporary overturning of the certainties we believed in as children, thus forming a thematic link with 'Rondo for Eamonn'.

The four stanzas of the poem in strict rhyme (ABACBC) are musically observed in Bodley's setting, thereby making the musical irony more poignant. Each stanza opens a variant of the opening line, where the star is brought into focus: 'Where is the star that winks in the east'; in stanza two it 'signals', in stanza three it 'beckons', and in the final stanza it 'dances'. Within this framework the poet is always searching for something – 'some star to blink beyond doubt' (l.6) or a request for daily bread (l.15) – or making pleas reminiscent of late Kavanagh: 'Find me a crèche where a God is cradled by woman's arm' (l.18); and later 'O give us our innocence all green and eager' (l.23). Both adult and child on Christmas Eve, he is 'reconciled to bear this double witness to a mystery' (l.12), and in the parallel lines of the final stanza he raises his glass 'to the God of renewal'. The contrasting moods of Bodley's setting hinge on how his reading of O'Siadhail's text is to be understood. Is the falling star a musical icon of the birth of Christ or an expression of existential uncertainty? Does this musical motif bear 'double witness' to the mysteries of O'Siadhail's text, depending on how the star motif is performed? From his opening musical statement, expressive but not florid (bars 302-3), Bodley expresses a certain doubt, which reappears in the *stringendo* request for 'some star to blink beyond a doubt'. The accompanying syncopations in stanza two signal uncertainty poignantly resting on an A minor chord, one of the rare moments in the cycle where simple tonality is used to make a strong musical statement,[24] stressing the element of chance in our fate (bars 321-22). Bodley's setting is interwoven with musical contradictions: the *stringendo* and ascending dynamic statement of the poet's reconciliation to bear 'double witness to a mystery', doubled in the bass, is immediately answered by a mere allusion to the star (bar 326). Although the images of bread and wine are more solidly backed by the piano (bars 331-33) and the birth of Christ accompanied by very simple chording, almost resembling an organ accompaniment in F major, the consecutive minor chords which follow are unexpected in their sequence, rather like Gesualdo though in a different context. Similarly the *mezzoforte* statements of the poet's plea for innocence and the ascending dynamics of the final salutation are musically ambiguous. The song ends on a hesitant note: in the last appearance of the star the music is curtailed: suggestion rather than statement.

'Debonair'
In the next four songs of the cycle O'Siadhail explores the vicissitudes of love in a style utterly his own and introduces the richly ambiguous texture and hypnotic rhythms which are central to his poetry. The first of these settings, 'Debonair', is a delicate, limpid, small-scale miniature, only two pages long, in which Bodley raises nuance to extreme heights. The song opens with a recurring idea of forceful trills with contrary movement that runs through the accompaniment and mirrors the celebration of life in the poem. The expressive melodic movement is exchanged with stepwise movement and repeated notes to highlight musically the panache of poetic images, 'a carnation raffish in her ebony hair' and 'a riptide of energy'. The piano illustration of 'a waking flower' with rising thirds' (bars 364-68) which recurs in 'Hovering', or the sudden switch to an F major tonal centre for 'the homegoers pass by' (bar 377), are examples of the natural hierarchy of the relationship between voice and accompaniment and some of the ways in which intimacy presides in Bodley's settings of O'Siadhail. Such small changes of melodic contour and harmony alter mood and declamation subtly but unmistakably.

'Hurt'
'Hurt' is one of O'Siadhail's rare expressions of a poetics of dissonance, the discords of which are made in response to a lover who double-crosses. The prelude begins with gently dissonant *pianissimo* chords, an echo of the technique used at the beginning of the cycle, now used to herald the longing and frustrations of the human heart. Bodley's setting suitably affords the singer ample scope for intense expression, with its speech-like rhythms, rubato tempo and careful vocal registration. From the beginning of the song, narration in the vocal line draws us into a tale that is graphically illustrated by the piano. The expressive rising vocal line and accompaniment, 'I warmed, I opened, I yielded, I loved', form a strong contrast to the strong delivery of 'You of all people to double cross!' In this setting Bodley assigns to the singer's speaking register parlando passages that bear important text. The speech rhythm used in 'Intimacy cuts both ways' and 'that way you'd have called its tune' transfers the narrative character of the poem into subjective expression. These passages of musical soliloquy stand out especially when one realizes that these are the composer's readings of these lines. Although he mirrors O'Siadhail's prosody in the rhythm of the vocal lines, Bodley has the ability to make speech-like vocal lines psychologically vivid. Part of the force of this musical soliloquy is its softness and powerful lowering of the dynamics. As the voice is almost reduced to narration, a new accompaniment figuration emerges in the piano part (bar 395) which gives full lyrical expression to the passion of the moment. So too the six bars of descending minor triads, a chromatic descent from g minor to b minor in the bass, beautifully point the protagonist's admission: 'But I know I know nothing. All that is certain is change.' The protagonist's recognition of life's flux is symbolized in the return of the opening two chords, parts of which are now exchanged between treble and bass and descend chromatically until the music dies away.

'Return'

In *The Naked Flame* O'Siadhail subtly suggests that the world of appearances – the phenomenal or representational world as Kant and Schopenhauer call it – is not the only existence. In the closing lines of 'Hurt' he suggests a higher existence, a hidden reality, which can reveal itself to those who dare to take risks, who dare to live fully. Here in 'Return' O'Siadhail's title symbol, *The Naked Flame*, serves as a catalyst which conjures up in sound, image, or feeling, the suggestion of a hidden reality. And in the closing lines of this poem, the poet illuminates what lies beyond the veil, an inner reality:

> Wait! Supposing, how can we be sure?
> I shy from fire. You insist I drop veil
> After veil; we stand before the naked flame.

Bodley recognizes the existence beyond the representational world which O'Siadhail evokes in this poem and conveys its essence through musical symbols.[25] O'Siadhail imbues the poems of *The Naked Flame* with the suggestiveness he holds to be the privilege of music[26] and in this setting Bodley luxuriates in music's supreme power to suggest. Musical suggestion provides him with the key to hidden reality; in this setting he creates an aura of subtle mystery and expressive ambiguity, an introspective style that suggests rather than defines.

O'Siadhail intentionally isolates and thereby stresses the idea of return – 'the finesse of rebeginnings!' – the initial words of the supposed statement of solace and return. Bodley composes a musical parallel by immediately evoking this idea of return through a musical matrix where the music passes in effect from 4/4 to 5/4 to 4/4 to establish a seemingly indeterminate rhythm. Through these changes of time signature, he continually modifies the refined but pert pace of 'Return', replacing the regular 4/4 bars with bars of 5 beats, inscribing in his notation a liquid rhythmic flow, unhampered by any regularity of pulsation. Bodley creates this kind of rhythm through a double time signature, changing dynamics, and the kind of rhythmic configurations consigned to the pianist. The accompaniment returns all the time over the same passage, under a voicing of the same melodic phrase. This motif is altered and repeated less rigidly in the second strophe until the keyword, 'become', is signalled by F sharp: a subtle resounding of the tonal centre of the 'double loss of faith before gain' ('In those we follow', bar 263). Bodley observes O'Siadhail's notion of becoming with a change to a *mezzoforte subito* marking a more hopeful note, a modulation to B flat and a different type of accompaniment figuration (bar 440). Such close textual reading is evident through his setting as related literary lines share musical images, 'I hankered after you' echoes 'we angle between the coyness of once intimates' (bar 429). At bar 473 the left hand shifts down to figuration which is closer to the very opening of the work, this time with particular reference to the second chord of bar 1: a musical intimation of the naked flame, intensified by the contrasting bars and ascending dynamics of 475 and 479. The cycle's title image, 'the naked flame', is answered in the postlude with the twelve notes which open and close the piece: a voicing which demands a performance with panache.

'Love-song'

O'Siadhail shares with Bodley a fundamental music aesthetic: namely, music's ability to speak to us most directly.[27] In 'Love-song' O'Siadhail achieves his own unique blend of precision and sublimity. What is crucial to the lines, and also to the entire cycle, is the sense of joy and confidence imparted by the inner melody, the middle voice, which finds expression in the exquisite movement of the lines: a dance of beatitude sustained to the end of the poem. O'Siadhail's meaning is carried by the dancing effect of this highly wrought musical poem, which manages to concede the ephemerality of love at the same time as it celebrates its reality.

Bodley's rendering of 'Love-song' alternates parlando and rhythmical singing in a continuous flow, as if the singer were alternating between factual description and expression of feeling.[28] Bodley's speech-like styles in this cycle are as protean as they are polymorphic. Here in 'Love-song' his vocal writing is marked by shifts in a continuum that move quite seamlessly from modern lyrical melody to intensified speech. In this modern lyrical setting, he imparts to a handful of phrases the suggestion of speech in order to draw attention to these phrases, in particular, highlighting the central theme in stanza three: 'half of what we love is love's fragility', where the accompaniment is reduced to a bare minimum. Against this vocal alternation the accompaniment flows continuously like a countermelody: counter to the melodic content and changes. There is always something shifting in a linear manner, moving constructively to carry the music through those passages so that the quasi-parlando phrases are run against something continuous to carry the musical movement forward. Good examples of this are the additive structure in the treble at bar 502 which expands into a slow movement of thirds, enabling musical continuity to take place as the voice switches to quasi-parlando or the portrayal of autumn (bars 528-29). Such use of subtle transitions between speaking and singing gives a musical character to these passages of intensified speech.

O'Siadhail's strict rhyme, which runs through the four seasons of the poem, is mirrored by the imaginative motivic structures of the setting. The song opens with a slow triplet motif in the bass developed through the first stanza; a portrayal of early spring. Descending thirds, which portray the poignant symbol of a snowdrop, a harbinger of hope, spiral at bar 508 to illustrate O'Siadhail's personification. They announce the arrival of summer (bars 516-19) where 'summer lush and unplanned' is accompanied by one of the rare moments of simple tonality in the cycle: the lush chord of E major. With the arrival of autumn and transition into winter the triplet idea is expanded into chillier fourths (bars 532 and 543). The closing image, 'A scent lingers', is related to the fragrances in 'Tuning In' (bar 42), a musical reference which is not in the poetry.

'A Closure'

A powerfully dramatic song, dense in texture, now makes its climactic appearance. This song of lost love and human longing traverses the stages of grief following the loss of one deeply loved, attempting to make sense of such loss. The general tenor of O'Siadhail's poem calls for Bodley's strong musical expression. The vocal line is chromatic, rich in modern lyricism and, especially in dramatic passages, of extensive range. The piano part is expressively chromatic and wide-ranging; the setting is rhythmically enriched and hinges around quite sharp harmonies.

Dramatic descriptive music abounds. The song hinges around the original two chords, symbols of past and future, restated like a thunderclap at the beginning to herald the protagonist's loss. The rich dramatic refinement of the writing is evident in the opening stanza, reflective in tone. In 'Captive in the lurch, my heart rebels', voice and dynamic continually rise and drop until the striking *fortissimo chord* is announced in the rebellion of 'unseized chances' (bar 564). Here Bodley sets the significant passage, 'But no, I won't mourn', to the highest pitch heard so far in the song, which brings these words into special prominence. The voice falls back in pitch and dynamics to settle momentarily on 'Nothing and everything', where the sense of loss is evoked through the chromaticism.

A dramatic oscillation of musical moods mirrors O'Siadhail's portrayal of grief. And Bodley gives such images of darkness and daybreak a double meaning. In the closing lines of stanza three he takes pains to develop the question, 'What do I do with all this love?' into a soaring melodic line which commences on a high D flat, a step lower than the last cry of anguish, which the soloist is left to carry alone against a held chord. Swiftly the mood changes, 'So lightly you'd quipped', deliberately moving into a simple accompaniment, which commences with a lighter texture of descending 6ths, but changes to a suggestion of anguish (bar 575). Bodley's accompanying figurations parallel

O'Siadhail's evocation of meanings achieved by assembling unresolved questions and contrasting blocks of images in the text. 'My boat of moods lunges forward'[29] the singer proclaims *fortissimo* as the music is reduced to a dramatic hold on one note, setting a platform to accentuate her isolation: 'Then, just dallying alone'. This oscillation between dynamic extremes intensifies in the final stanzas which are closely unified motivically. The *piano* voicing of temporary solace, 'I calm, touching down where we'd been together', is underscored by the same chording as directly before, so too 'I'll ripen in my sorrow', is underscored by referral to this earlier portrayal of solace (bars 587-90). Poignant interruptions of the past are symbolized by a modified return of the opening chord of the work at bar 591, where the opening bass chord now resounds in the treble, combined with the right hand chord at the end of bar 1. Hollow octaves in the dark recesses of the piano (bar 594) accompany the singer's winter's journey, suggesting the murky twilight and pain of sleeplessness. The brightening passage 'I'll ripen in my sorrow' evokes not only a feeling of daybreak but the feeling of torment gradually eased. Bodley soothes the feverish spasms into peaceful pulsations before the song's close– a musical parallel of the hope O'Siadhail casts in the poem's conclusion. The rhetorical question: 'But no, I won't mourn why should I?' is granted a musical reply: 'I'll search for you in every face.' And the vocal line is filled with all the sorrow these words can convey. The intensity of the central motif throbs feverishly at the song's close.

'Initiation'

Bodley picks up on O'Siadhail's chiasma between 'Rondo for Eamonn' and 'Initiation' by composing a recurring rondo idea, a pentatonic tune and salient triplet theme, answered by descending fourths. This undulating triplet figure parallels the mood of the poem, a poetic scene where the poet is talking to a boy over a game of cards. Bodley opens this scene with an expression of naturalism in music. The quotidian image of dealing cards is almost spoken, answered by the speech rhythms of dialogue, which requires crisp enunciation and vivid representation of the words. The youthful enthusiasm of a child and the passing of time are captured by the spirit of the music, which is continually moving forward. This feeling is augmented by the changing time signatures from 3/4 to 2/4 to 3/4 to 2/4 in the melody against passages of descending fourths: 'All moods flit across your eye' (bars 655-658). O'Siadhail's clinching statement, 'Should you not keep such innocence', is heralded by hollow octaves and answered with descending fourths, a musical motif carried over from 'Love-song' where they marked the passing of time; here they allude to the loss of childhood and youthful enthusiasms. Transformed in this song, they draw attention to the vulnerability of the child and the realization that you cannot take this gift away. 'As in 'Rondo for Eamonn' the future becomes an unreadable kind of open book. 'Your road out, my road back': Bodley's pointing of these words clinches one of O'Siadhail's many reconciliations of tensions and opposites crucial to the poet's celebration of being. The song closes with the boy's story in the future and a childhood waiting to be regained.

'Hovering'

In *The Naked Flame* the poet's vitalism offers ways of unchaining our description of individuality from the limiting, formal concepts of person, and in 'Hovering' (no.11) O'Siadhail perceives the expanding centre of a human character, a woman's rediscovery of love. This penultimate poem imparts the sense of entering a new phase in one's life which produces a joy and fear essential to the intensification of the poet's art. Bodley's richly expressive song of human longing is concerned with fairly clear-cut chording. The thirds idea in 'Debonair' returns here with a different meaning; this time to portray a mature woman falling in love again. The thirds rise against static chords on the beat to prepare the vocal entry, 'Watch those eyes', beautifully pointed by larger intervals of the phrase. Wide leaps of great intensity in this song, 'I drown in his glance' and 'Can this be me?', catch the movement of these phrases. This movement in sevenths permeates the last stanza and becomes an expression of embraced uncertainty.

In 'Hovering' Bodley captures the psychological overtones in his characterization – the woman's inner agitation, her vacillation, her growing courage and finally her fixed determination to embrace the unknown. The broad intervals of the opening lines portray her inner feeling. Sudden changes of dynamics show her changing moods: her caution is conveyed through the double *piano* markings of 'Surely that was an age ago' (bars 688-89) and the *mezzopiano* voicing of 'Still I hover like a fledgling'; her ascending courage, marked by the *forte* statement, 'I dare what I never dared then', is almost a reflective comment (bars 703-5), while the ascending vocal inflection of 'I relearn doubts and jealousy, a debutante craving the fitful ebbs and flows of sweet madness of first ecstasy' portrays her courage finally at its height. Bodley marks this inner transformation with a change in the accompaniment, giving it a very strong *espressivo* in the slowly-spread *pp* chords (bar 716). The sway of feeling of the opening lines returns in wide leaps of the final stanza with full emphasis on her embrace of love's uncertainty: 'swaying on hinges of our everyday'. The song is thus a fine example of how Bodley sets repeated verbal phrases differently to reflect the particular shade of meaning each phrase acquires as a result of its changing position in the poetic context.

'Rhapsody'

For Rheinhold Brinkmann, one definition of musical modernism is a 'critical, almost enigmatic relationship between allegorical (non-representational) and symbolic (representational) language'.[30] This recognition of the non-representational and the representational lies behind the philosophical poems which frame *The Naked Flame*. Bodley's musical rendering achieves such equipoise. The final song opens with a triple statement of the second chord of bar 1, a musical symbol of the past and a recognition of the poetic chiasma between these two poems. Bodley's rendering of the opening stanza is a musical allegory of life's flux. The continual movement in the long vocal phrases and changing accompaniment figurations comes to rest on the poet's commentary on the human condition. 'Though we search for footholds in what was or will be' is granted a simple musical statement, so too the rejection of equilibrium in favour of trust in 'the love that is surrender to the flow' is beautifully pointed in the vocal line by the octave leap to a high 'G' on 'love': a thematic reference to the poetic ideas of the opening stanza. In 'all this flux ... some patterns form', a new figuration in bar 769 accompanying the musical flux is answered by a richly expressive recitative to embody the absolute climax of the poem: 'Yet you are never there, never have arrived', its musical message underscored by contrary motion linear movement in the piano's middle voice. The additive structures of 'Love-song' (bar 502) recur to underscore the mores of human activity. As the song moves into an intensely dramatic vocal codetta, Bodley breaks with conventional limitations on expression and repeatedly replaces one tempo and dynamic marking with another, the aim being to breathe the fiery presence of electrifying performance into his score. The song depends on the singer reaching a very intense degree of expression. Bodley leaves the singer on her own against held chords, musically pointing how we are 'vulnerable to how it is' in life. Patches of light colour, punctuated by off-beat pulsations suggest the natural images to follow, which singer and pianist must have courage to perform. The major 9ths which underscore 'the love that is forever in motion' are deliberately stellar. The airy shapelessness of the song's first half is distilled at its close in a passage firmly rooted in the musical symbols of *The Naked Flame*. As the poem speaks of the mystery of the moment, the cycle ends with a soft statement of the two chords with which it opened.

Earlsfort Suite

The *Earlsfort Suite* was part of the cultural project, *Ceoil Reoite*, led by Dúchas (The Heritage Service) for the Millenium year. Taking Goethe's famous quote, 'Architektur ist gefrorene Musik' (Architecture is frozen music),[31] as the starting point, Dúchas commissioned a series of works to commemorate historic buildings in Ireland. As with *The Naked Flame*, this cycle began its musical life as a joint commission by RTÉ of both poetry and music for a new orchestral song cycle by Seóirse Bodley to commemorate the National Concert Hall.[32] The trilogy O'Siadhail produced, the *Earlsfort Suite*, is brilliantly apposite to the commission. In this cycle O'Siadhail plays upon the immediacy of music, its unrivalled power to recall and awaken definite associations, which enables him to bring into the present truths of feeling essential to the poem's transcendence of time. Under the sway of music, the poet moves from the actualities of the living present into a remote past, the scene of his birth at the Stella Maris Home on Earlsfort Terrace in January 1947. O'Siadhail's evocative listing of events in 'Delivery' offers the poet a way of banishing the present and revisiting this time. In 'Rites of Passage', music is again identified with a power to overcome time as the poet recalls the concert hall's former existence as an examination hall and relives the terror of this scene. The private and the public are brought together in the final poem, where, for all the undisclosed and inconclusive aspects, we detect the charm that Earlsfort Terrace holds for O'Siadhail. Taken as a whole, the three poems span a gap between intimate losses and more public, shared experiences of history's passing, touching upon music's intimacy with our long developing and changing culture.

Bodley's fascination with the expressive potential of the orchestra began with his first orchestral song cycle, *Never to have lived is best*, five Yeats's songs for soprano and orchestra, composed in 1965.[33] In this early cycle Bodley began to cultivate orchestral song whose musical imagery serves to mirror the poetic symbolism, an artistic approach again adopted in the *Earlsfort Suite*. Although conceived for the concert hall rather than private performance, the *Earlsfort Suite* was characteristically written in short score, which the composer then orchestrated. In the orchestration of his keyboard version Bodley made no structural alterations; he wished to be faithful to the original and simply to shade it more delicately. The first example encountered is the use of solo strings with hand-muted stopped brass and a suspended cymbal murmuring softly in the background (bar 3). Subtle changes in orchestra are again noted at figure A (bar 14), where three solo violins are answered by *tutti* strings delicately accompanied by harp with muted trumpets *pppp* backing the solo strings, while muted French horns *ppp* back the tutti strings. In 'Rite of Passage', Bodley's orchestration of high flutes and piccolos answered by *sul ponticello* violins 1 and 2 (bars 76-77) creates an unearthly platform for the singer to re-enter the scene.

Typical pianistic figurations, found occasionally in the piano accompaniment, were effectively translated into orchestral timbre, an example of which is found in the woodwind rendition of the semiquaver figuration in 'Delivery', (bar 34). Further examples are the violin *glissandi* in 'Rite of Passage' (bar 65); the harmonics in solo strings (bar 66); or the flute and piccolo voicings of the demi-semiquaver figurations over bowed tremolo in the strings (bars 67 and 71).

In writing for voice and orchestra Bodley was very conscious of the proper balance and so the cycle unfolds a subtle development of musical idea and he orchestrates with a light hand. Rather than weave vast orchestral fabrics, Bodley spun delicate chamber music textures against the vocal line and only allows the orchestra prominence in the gaps between poetic lines.[34] The instrumental web of this orchestral setting brings the voice graciously into prominence. It also allows for balance between the intimate context of the text and orchestral accompaniment. Bodley's orchestral cycle contains fine distinctions of intensity. Nuance is of the greatest importance. Bodley notates dynamic nuance, examples of which are in 'Delivery' at 'gathering snow' (bar 13) marked by *pppp* trumpets, balanced by triple *piano con sordini* horns, or the *fp* strings which respond to the reappearance of the Fates in 'Rite of Passage' (bar 115). His songs show consummate skill with the lightest kinds of colouring, an example of which is the solo woodwind voicing over a string tremolo (bars 91-96): here the orchestral web is even lighter than the piano version. In 'Streetscape' one feels the living presence of the street in the first *tutti* passage of the cycle (bars 121-22) and directly after 'as the city begins to grow and boom' (bar 132). In general Bodley prefers to suggest mood rather than detail imagery, yet he also orchestrated the particell to sharpen the imagery of the songs. In 'Rite of Passage', 'same maze of a nightmare' is brought into prominence by *sul ponticello* strings (bars 107-08) and, in 'Streetscape', 'a silence of nervous memory echoes in its walls' is underscored by hushed arco strings' with an implied echo in the *pianissimo* timpani roll (bars 147-48). For the poetic lines which close this song Bodley mixes wind hues and colours on a refined orchestral palette (bars 149-168) which expands in the orchestral postlude that crescendos to triple *forte* in the final bars. These songs display his supreme command of orchestral sonority. Orchestral timbre enriches the lyricism of the original piano version, deepening sentiment and heightening mood.

'Delivery'
'Delivery' presents a view of Dublin, of its actuality in the light of the past, which is moving and direct. It is striking that O'Siadhail neither invests Dublin with a poignant atmosphere of certain loss nor, like Behan, laments a lost locality. Instead, in the *Earlsfort Suite*, O'Siadhail recalls a culture that has disappeared and validates its existence in the act of recording it. In its intimations of transformation and tradition, O'Siadhail's Dublin possesses a spirit of place able to offer all the consolations a poetry of place customarily involves in Irish cultural tradition with all its suggestions of belonging, of familial and local continuities. The city shows its character in O'Siadhail's language and diction, the realist vernacular style championed by Kavanagh, both contemporary and unaffected, and whose range of reference embraces popular as much as high culture. Yet in contrast to Kavanagh's ruralization of Baggot Street and the area around the canal – and indeed all writers who have rendered the city as text before him – O'Siadhail anchors the old stereotype of a literary Dublin in a musical location. His evocation of Earlsfort Terrace becomes a complex way of Irish belonging, of remembering, of situating himself in a local cultural terrain, though his significance lies in the poetic validation of his home ground in a wider European context. O'Siadhail's validation of this complex European inheritance places his poetic record in radical contrast to the Dublin of George Moore's *A Drama in Muslin*, written a hundred years earlier or the recent Grafton Street setting of the story, 'Parachutes', by John McGahern, who does not cast Dublin as a European city. O'Siadhail's Dublin is, in fact, closer to the representation of the Irish capital in *Ulysses* and *Finnegan's Wake* by Joyce who treats his city as a site of vernacular modernism without the defining conditions of modernity – exile, isolation, and questions of identity. Indeed, the sweep of history embraced by Joyce's belief, 'if I can get to the heart of Dublin, I can get to the heart of the world' is here extended by O'Siadhail to include 'the heart of myself'. 'Song leads us home to where we have not yet been', George Steiner believes,[35] and in the *Earlsfort Suite* O'Siadhail never lets his own life slip too far away from the life of a particular time and place. To borrow Louis MacNeice's words, the poems become both 'a panorama and a confession of faith' in a changing city.[36]

The truth for O'Siadhail, as for any poet, has to be his own truth: an expression of the unique relation between the poet and Earlsfort Terrace, as he traces Dublin's history in the lineaments of his own life. The poem becomes a record of personal experience realized in poetry and reveals the rhythm of the historical moment: the transformation of Dublin city into a European capital in one lifetime and the global well-spring of the self in endless play. In 'Delivery' the poet's ears are filled with the voices of 1947 which he notes with a continual shifting of tone. O'Siadhail has always been a musical poet, and here he has devised the harmonic scale of a new era. The poem makes a profound response to a changing Dublin, and expresses its emotional content with extraordinary power. The testimony of 'Delivery' is to O'Siadhail's birth year that provides him with a series of recurring and compelling images which transcend the self so that his subject matter becomes the history of his own time or generation and the history of times remote from his own. From the snow of 1947 which swept across America and lasted in Ireland for a long time[37] to the 'new look' in women's clothes (a signal that the world was out of the war) – these emblems of 1947 contribute to O'Siadhail's 'voice' as poet, to the haunted and understated qualities in his writing, and to the voice's responsibility in relation to the seriousness of what it records. The poem becomes a kaleidoscope of associations and transformations in Dublin, raising the question of what – if anything – remains stable in the island of the self.

In contrast to *The Naked Flame*, the earlier piano song cycle by Bodley and O'Siadhail, this poetic trilogy is deliberately shorter and so does not contain the same variety of moods. Accordingly their musical form is less varied than the earlier settings. Nos.1 and 3 are ♩=60 and based on a descending figure of thirds. (The central song is only a little faster.) Such musical borrowing between songs lends the cycle a definite musical perspective, with musical contrast occurring within this architectural musical frame. Bodley's setting of O'Siadhail's Wordsworthian sonnet,[38] 'Delivery' (of a child), introduces the main musical motif on which the cycle is based. In 'Delivery' a tertial motif makes its appearance as an underlying series of superimposed thirds, which do not descend sequentially, but rather twist and turn within this ambit:

Example 3: Bodley, *Earlsfort Suite*, 'Delivery' (no.1), piano, bars 1-2

Example 4: Bodley, *Earlsfort Suite*, 'Delivery' (no.1), voice, bars 4-13

Between bars 4 and 13, the interval of ascending or descending thirds continually expands while the piano's left hand plots permutations of the descending tone.

In the *Earlsfort Suite* subtle dissonance which colours the expression occurs along with motivic manipulation – both of which are demonstrated by the impressive 'Delivery'. In bar 10 of this song, the secondary seventh on B flat is contradicted by the B natural in the treble, an example of piquant dissonance idiomatic to this expression. Bodley heightens this image of the three 'bronze Fates', a recurring image in O'Siadhail's verse,[39] by adding the note 'B flat' to the series of superimposed thirds at 'spin'. Bodley answers and illustrates this literary idea with textual imagery in the piano part: a spinning or linking movement in the bass and a subtle use of musical illustration. Though the music returns to its subtle play on intervals of a third, it swiftly shifts to the idea of gathering snow, where the harmonic shift to D flat, takes us in a different direction and the accompaniment settles on a musical metaphor of falling snow. Over this gentle accompaniment O'Siadhail's listing of events in 1947 commences with the notes of a minor 7th chord of F. For Bodley, such naming of objects – a local example of which is found in Joyce's *Ulysses*[40] – produces a variety of moods conjuring up a time and place; the reference to women's clothing granting it a gentle ironic tone. In his music Bodley plays with O'Siadhail's language but the play is serious in intent, as the composer defines and explores his musical voice under its guidance. Examples are found in varied musical images, where the vocal nadir at 'G' heightens the ascending melisma on 'Hekla's fire'. Here Bodley's subtle use of musical rhythm on 'Hekla's fire' and 'desire' provides the singer ample opportunity to infuse emotive words with feelings. He highlights these emotive words with melismas and also in an entirely different manner by underscoring them with pungent harmony: a passage of dissonant chromaticism in bar 22 where an augmented chord in the treble is underscored by a diminished chord and finds its echo in the diminished triad with an added third at bar 29. The introductory motif returns in bar 30 where the tertial idea is developed in both hands before the musical motif recurs in a higher octave, signalling the reflective mood to follow. Its second reappearance in bars 47-49 reaches a new apex of dissonance. The poetic image of falling snow recurs to portray 'a lava of pure desire' heightened by chromaticism in bar 51 (E flat instead of the expected E natural) and bar 56 (A flat instead of A natural). This descending vocal line of superimposed thirds is beautifully answered by the final ascent of Bodley's opening metaphor: G (bar 60) to B (bar 61) to D (bar 62) to F sharp (bar 63) as the top two notes of the series resound in the final bar. The unfolding of this musical motif forms a musical image of the notion of becoming, the music offering a specific case of this general concept in practice.

'Rite of Passage'
The willingness to juxtapose the value and power of art in relation to the demands of reality has been part of the rhetoric of poetry for centuries but has come into renewed focus in the twentieth century. In 'Rite of Passage' the eternal world of art exists in relation to the temporal as O'Siadhail travels from the artistic world of the concert hall to revisit its former existence as an examination hall of University College Dublin. As in the opening poem of the cycle, this poem remains true to the experiences of O'Siadhail's youth – and mankind's youth – before the march of knowledge, experience, and history. The poet's recollection of sitting 'a passage of unseen' Latin subtly unveils the hidden contours of a vanishing world[41] as he glances forward to the later use of the space as a concert hall, encompassing within his own growth and sophistication, that of a musical tradition within his native city. O'Siadhail's use of a past literary source, Flann O'Brien's image of the living chessboard,[42] makes further reference to a bygone age. Such bi-focal vision gives tremendous poignancy to these poems that establish an equilibrium between past and present, loss and gain.

In 'Rite of Passage' Bodley exploits music's supreme expressiveness to create an evocative atmosphere of an exam scene and to place the protagonist in this life-like setting. In the opening lines Bodley sets up a play of major and minor tonalities which mirrors the uncertainties of O'Siadhail's opening imagery: 'nervous last minute tips', 'high-strung recall'. In the prelude to these bars Bodley creates an illusion of reality by painting a scene in the piano part with descriptive music. Musically this song refers to nos.1 and 3 as the opening motif is based on thirds, though subtly disguised by Bodley's use of fifths and percussive rhythm.

Example 5: Bodley, *Earlsfort Suite*, 'Rite of Passage' (no.2), piano, bar 64

Bodley uses this implied sequence emphasizing the nervous 'high-strung' quality of the fifths. More than any other O'Siadhail setting the opening passage here musically alludes to the avant garde: Bodley's slight recall to render the poem's nervous tone. This song is also a fine example of musical portraiture which illustrates Bodley's ability to capture psychological overtones in his musical characterization. The poet's agitation and temporary anxiety are vividly portrayed by the syncopations in the opening phrase and sudden changes of dynamics. Bodley raises the threshold of inner torment to higher levels by distorting the vocal line with wide leaps of great intensity. The two staccato notes in the vocal line answered by a descent based around the figuration of thirds (bars 73 and 74) suggest an expression of extreme tension. This mood is intensified by the rapid vocal crescendo on '(last minute) tips' over B flat major underscored by B natural in bar 74. So too the idea of 'high-strung recall' is represented in a catatonic way (bars 77-79) – a direct contrast to the musical surrealism suggested in bars 84 to 87, where the threatening image of a disinterested attendant administering exam papers – a scene frozen in time – lies behind Bodley's elongated phrase accompanied by hollow octaves. The 'hushed silence' of the setting is signalled by a *fortepiano* dynamic and agitated chromaticism of the accompaniment which underscores the 'passage of unseen' culminating in a *fortepiano* passage to parallel the poem's turbulence. Or does it draw our attention to the passage of time, subtly marked by recurring but altered thirds, which herald the transformation of the hall and the self? The mounting tension of O'Siadhail's recurring adult dream is announced musically by the return of the accompanying figuration. The return of this motif bears testimony to Bodley's ability to set repeated phrases differently to reflect the particular shade of meaning each phrase acquires as a result of its changing position in the poetic context. The piano thunders in this climactic passage until the ascending lines of pianist and singer alike reflect anguish never relieved. The augmented triads of bars 107 and 110, and the atmospheric descent in the left hand at 'same maze of a nightmare', followed by the deliberate clashes between voice and accompaniment, intensify the poetic scene before we are led back to the poetic image of the Fates by Bodley's introductory idea of thirds: a deliberate development of the opening ideas of this musical trilogy.

'Streetscape'
The final song of the *Earslfort Suite* moves into the National Concert Hall, its former life and memories contained in it. In rendering so clearly an urban landscape left behind, the poet evokes a sense of where the city is now. As in the 'Wandering Rocks' chapter of Joyce's *Ulysses*, a Dublin streetscape is portrayed as a scene of sociability and excitement. Here the street is depicted as the seat of competing activities, motivations and forces, many of which are propelled by cars, and from which the concert hall offers sanctuary. In this existence of endless movement, we are reminded of the importance of human individuality in an urban environment.

Bodley takes his cue from the literary theme of life's transience, the flow of time, as the poetic images float over a structure of thirds, which bring with it a circular unity. Bodley's subtle transformation of this recurring musical motif, takes its cue from Heraclitus' famous maxim, 'You can't step into the same river twice' – only here it is the same musical water: the river is always there, yet transformed. Here Bodley's triadic chords which open and close, and underscore a vocal line in thirds, result in a resonant harmony and style of movement related to the opening movement. So too the musical imagery on 'Hekla's fire' and 'desire' (bars 19-22; 25-28) is echoed in 'remembrance and desire'. Bodley's flowing figuration at bar 128 signals the poet's recognition of the flow of time; so too the falling motif of the opening song is used differently and the harmonic centre shifts in recognition of a vanishing scene of the poet's birth. Bodley's music seems to intensify the sense of being in a changing world and produces the musical emotions essential to the intensification of the poet's art. Here the recollection of the examination hall is voiced *mezzopiano* in direct contrast to the *forte* images of the concert hall. Such dynamic shifts continue as the music is thinned out to capture the image of a hushed audience at a concert and the echo of nervous memory in its walls. As the poet contemplates such change, the vocal line moves in quiet contemplation, a movement poignantly underscored by an ostinato of set notes in irregular patterns. Bodley's asymmetric repetitions of such patterns overlap in the piano and voice or within the piano part itself, dovetailing the close of one phrase with the beginning of another. The result is a thick, interlaced texture and continuity of movement which is allowed to die out in a subtle allusion to the flux of time. Bodley's vocal codetta functions as a continuation and gradual dissipation of the atmosphere of the poem –a refinement in expression used by the late Romantics, who favoured the hushed conclusion. Like a twist of fate, Bodley's closing gestures, an exploitation of dynamic extremes and free allusion to the opening chords, catch us by surprise as the piano crescendoes into a surge of sound, and the song fulminates at triple *forte*.

Musical Images and Identity
Taken together, the songs of the *Earlsfort Suite* are more than the sum of their parts, transcending the 'occasional' category as individual instances of memory and commemoration of an historical building and the millennium year, and accumulating into a wider perspective on cultural history. In their blend of personal and historical, these imaginative settings point towards the release of *Globe* and the music of Bodley's most recent period. To explore in these works such questions of identity, we must consider identity not only in the sense of personal hallmarks of both artists but also as an indication of the internal consistency of a work. Bodley's O'Siadhail settings are examples of free configurations, where the musical form seems to depend almost entirely on the poetry for its coherence. The rich seriated structure of the *Earlsfort Suite* presents the essentials of the plot in striking brevity yet with living perceptibility. The unity and deep sense of feeling in *The Naked Flame* are provided by melody in each song. In both cycles Bodley aimed at unity and integration, both in fashioning single songs and integrating them into a coherent cycle.

What distinguishes Bodley's song cycles from the cycles of his contemporaries? What is the specific signature, the artistic and historic significance of these cycles? This is not so much a question of artistic quality. Certainly there is no question about the artistic superiority of Bodley's O'Siadhail cycles. Several other contemporary settings of O'Siadhail's poems display solid craftsmanship and an original tone. But this is not the difference in which I am interested. These other settings of O'Siadhail poetry hide the significant and representational aspects of the texts behind the norms of private performance: they domesticate the images through the moderating limits of conventional performance. There is no paradigmatic perspective. Only Bodley aims at constituting a paradigm. In other words, Bodley's cycle elevates the protagonist to a model of identification for a modern audience, raising the problematic state of subjectivity – namely, the crisis of identity and the cohesion of 'I' in an urban environment. The O'Siadhail cycles aim at this sense of history not only by the poet's construction of a narrative 'plot' but through the form, structure, symbol, and tone of their music. The music of these cycles comments on the narrative of O'Siadhail's texts, on the respective 'plots' of *The Naked Flame* and the *Earlsfort Suite*, and it is this self-reflection of the work of art which defines its historical position.

As contemporary cycles of the highest artistic degree, Bodley's *The Naked Flame* and *Earlsfort Suite* offer a historical diagnosis. This presents the poet as the witness to modern life, embodying contemporary concerns about the state of subjectivity in a modern metropolis. But it is also a critical commentary on itself, on its own representational intent. In an extreme state of self-reflection these cycles are music about its own presence, song as history. And the compositional means to achieve this is to construct a cycle as song about song, song about a specific musical tradition. In the opening paragraphs of this essay I explored the connection of these cycles with nineteenth-century German models, and have traced Bodley's continuation of this lyrical tradition; modern, certainly, but lyrical in the sense of the close connection of music and text common to this tradition. In following this trajectory I have traced techniques of thematic and motivic construction, textures, and gestures. There is not a single song of these cycles that is not interwoven into the musical matrix of its companion settings. Both cycles are tightly constructed in the manner of the main cycles of this tradition, from Schubert to Schoenberg. But as important as these connections with such models is the way in which these models are used. In an age in which the contemporary art song is granted only a minor role in modern concert life, Bodley's sense of history reaffirms the quest of song to voice contemporary truths. Beyond the fine aesthetic qualities of both poetry and music, it is this historical signification that makes Bodley's O'Siadhail cycles important human and artistic documents of contemporary times.

Lorraine Byrne Bodley
January 2008

---

[1] As I write I am struck by the parallel with Seamus Heaney's lecture for the Royal Irish Academy on 28 January 2007, *Holding Patterns, Arts, Letters and the Academy*, reflections on how the humanities inform consciousness and equip people as creatures of memory and reflection, *The Irish Times* 29 January 2008, p. 7.

[2] Micheal O'Siadhail, 'Introduction: *Miss Unfathomable*', *Poems 1975-1995* (Newcastle upon Tyne: Bloodaxe Books, 1999), pp. 15-16.

[3] On the last page of his essay 'Cultural Criticism and Society', written in 1949, first published in 1951, and collected in *Prisms* in 1955, Adorno writes that 'Even the most extreme consciousness of doom threatens to degenerate into idle chatter. Cultural criticism finds itself faced with the final stage of the dialectic of culture and barbarism. To write poetry after Auschwitz is barbaric.

And this corrodes even the knowledge of why it has become impossible to write poetry today.' Theodor Adorno, *Prisms,* translated by Samuel and Shierry Weber (Cambridge MA: Massachusetts Institute of Technology Press, 1967), p. 34. For recent discussion, see, for example, Klaus Hofmann, 'Poetry after Auschwitz – Adorno's Dictum', *German Life and Letters,* 58.2 (April 2005), pp. 182-194.
4 Ezra Pound, 'The Serious Artist' (1913) in *Literary Essays of Ezra Pound,* ed. T.S. Eliot (London: Faber & Faber, r1954), p. 9.
5 Johann Gottfried von Herder, *Volkslieder* (1778-79; second ed. of 1807 titled *Stimmen der Völker in Liedern*). Herder's opinion is frequently cited; see, for example, William A. Wilson, 'Herder, Folklore and Romantic Nationalism', *The Journal of Popular Culture* 6 (4), (1973), pp. 819–835.
6 Friedrich Nietzsche *The Birth of Tragedy* (1871).
7 Edward F. Kravitt, *The Lied: Mirror of Late Romanticism* (New Haven and London: Yale University Press, 1996), p. 34.
8 A further example is found in 'Hovering' (*The Naked Flame*): 'Watch those eyes' (bars 678-79), 'I drown in his glance' (bars 684-85), Then the dream grows and grows' (bars 718-20), and 'swaying on hinges of our everyday' (bars 724-27).
9 In *The Naked Flame,* for example, much of the melodic content is backed up in the accompaniment to give assistance to the singer. From the opening song of this cycle Bodley's subtle way of supporting the melody's contour and unifying voice and piano is notable. See, for example, how the C flat at 'aftertaste' is signalled by grace note B natural. Further examples include the passage beginning 'diminished chords poised between tonalities' (bars 81-90) where the line moves up in chromatic ascent, yet the doubling between piano and voice is rather less obvious because of the changing octaves in the left hand.
10 W.B. Yeats, *Autobiographies* (London: Macmillan, 1955).
11 W.B. Yeats, *Responsibilities: Manuscript Materials by W.B. Yeats* (1916), ed. William H. O'Donnell (New York: Cornell University Press, 2003).
12 T.S. Eliot, 'Yeats', from the first annual Yeats Lecture, delivered to the Friends of the Irish Academy at the Abbey Theatre, Dublin, in 1940.
13 John Keats's letters expound on his aesthetic theory of 'negative capability'. His theory was first expressed in a letter to his brothers, George and Thomas Keats, dated Sunday, 21 December 1817: 'I had not a dispute but a disquisition with Dilke, on various subjects; several things dovetailed in my mind, & at once it struck me, what quality went to form a Man of Achievement especially in literature & which Shakespeare possessed so enormously – I mean Negative Capability, that is when man is capable of being in uncertainties, Mysteries, doubts without any irritable reaching after fact & reason.' For further discussion see: Stanley A. Leavy, 'John Keats's Psychology of Creative Imagination', *Psychoanalytic Quarterly* 39 (1970), pp. 173-197.
14 The cycle was first performed in the National Concert Hall on 7 April 1988, performed by Bernadette Greevy (mezzo-soprano) and Mícheál O'Rourke (piano).
15 Most of the poems were published afterwards in *The Middle Voice* (1992). See Micheal O'Siadhail, *Poems 1975-1995* (Newcastle upon Tyne: Bloodaxe Books, 1999), pp. 138ff.
16 Cited in the composer's programme note on *The Naked Flame.*
17 Ibid.
18 T.S. Eliot, 'East Coker', *Four Quartets* (London: Faber and Faber, 1950), p. 15. The poem's opening line is a derivation of Mary Queen of Scots's motto: '*En ma fin est mon commencement*' (In my end is my beginning).
19 Cited in the composer's programme note on *The Naked Flame.*
20 Frank Delaney, *The Sunday Press* 24 June 1984. See David F. Ford, 'Life, Work, and Reception' in *Musics of Belonging* (Dublin: Carysfort Press, 2007), p. 18.
21 Arthur Schopenhauer, *Die Welt als Wille und Vorstellung,* vol.3 (Wiesbaden: Brockhaus, 1949), p. 310.

22 Goethe's comments are drawn from his letter to Adalbert Schöpke, 16. 2. 1818. Cited in Hedwig Walwei Wiegelmann, ed., *Goethes Gedanken über Musik* (Frankfurt am Main: Insel Verlag, 1985), p.140. *Weimarer Ausgabe* 29/7980, p. 74.
23 Correspondence between Micheal O'Siadhail and Lorraine Byrne Bodley, 25 January 2008.
24 The other examples in this cycle are: the very simple chords in 'A Toast on the Eve' (bars 341-43) and the E major chord in 'Love-song' (no.8), (bar 517).
25 This idea of art as a symbol of hidden reality is explored by German idealist philosophers from Fichte to Nietzsche. Schelling, for example, agreed that works of genius are clear revelations of the absolute; Hegel recognized art as the highest expression of it; for Schopenhauer 'the essential and the permanent of all phenomena of the world became visual art, poetry or music', *Die Welt als Wille und Vorstellung*, p. 217.
26 For a development of this idea see Lorraine Byrne Bodley, 'The Poetry of Musical Perception' in *Musics of Belonging: The Poetry of Micheal O'Siadhail* (Dublin: Carysfort Press, 2006), pp. 93-109.
27 Ibid.
28 Composer's programme note.
29 O'Siadhail's analogies between sailing and the moods prefigure the nautical imagery of later anthologies; see, for example, *Love Life* (Northumberland: Bloodaxe Books, 2005): 'Launch', pp. 37-38; 'Voyage', pp. 39-40'; 'Watch', pp. 51-52; 'About', pp. 53-55; 'Ten to Seven' (no.3), p. 59; 'At Sea', p. 108; 'Passage', p. 111.
30 Brinkmann, 'The Lyric as Paradigm: Poetry and the Foundation of Arnold Schoenberg's New Music' in *German Literature and Music: An Aesthetic Fusion 1890-1989*, eds Claus Reschke and Howard Pollack (Fink 1992), p. 115. Earlier in the essay Brinkmann explores this concept in greater scope. '*Die Moderne* is defined as a form of art that forges a merely illustrative relationship to a preceding reality and, in fact, seems to abandon completely the mimetic character of poetry; an art that displays a new consciousness of form penetrated by reflection ... and, above all, an art that reflects itself in itself ... The work of art of *Die Moderne* is self-referential and culminates in the concept and the realization of the 'absolute poem', ibid., p. 112.
31 Peter Eckermann, *Gespräche mit Goethe* (Stuttgart: Reclam, 1986), 23 March 1829, p. 340. 'Ich habe unter meinen Papieren ein Blatt gefunden wo ich die Baukunst eine erstarrte Musik nenne. Und wirklich, es hat etwas; die Stimmung, die von der Baukunst ausgeht, kommt dem Effekt der Musik nahe.' (I found a page among my papers where I refer to architecture as frozen music. And essentially there's something in it; the mood which emanates from architecture comes close to the effect of music.) Goethe's metaphor has been adopted by others. The philosopher, Friedrich Wilhelm Schelling, recognized cathedrals as 'gefrorene Musik' and as 'erstarrte Musik'. Among others, Palladio and Schopenhauer borrowed Goethe's metaphor, which has been handed down to the present day. To this idea O'Siadhail added the idea of architecture as the third skin; see, for example, Scott Drake, *The Third Skin: Architecture, Technology & Environment* (2007) which explores architecture's links with cultural identity.
32 Bodley's commissioned choral symphony, 'Ceol', had been the opening work of the first concert there in 1981. The state opening took place on Wednesday, 9 September 1981, followed by a repeat of the programme in a gala concert on 10 September 1981. The première of the *Earlsfort Suite* took place on 17 September 2000 in the National Concert Hall, Dublin. The work was performed by the RTÉ Concert Orchestra, conducted by Proinnsias O Duinn. The mezzo-soprano was Bernadette Greevy, to whom the work is dedicated.
33 The first performance took place in the St Francis Xavier Hall on Friday, 11 June 1965. The cycle was performed by the Radio Éireann Symphony Orchestra, conducted by Tibor Paul. The soprano was Veronica Dunne.
34 Examples of this in 'Delivery' are the bowed tremolos which underscore 'Hekla's fire' and 'desire' where sharp muted *sforzando* brass answer the voice. In 'Rite of Passage' brass *sforzandi* answer the arrival of a paper in Latin (bars 90-91) and the *tutti* passage at the beginning of 'Streetscape' (bars 121-22) is immediately reduced as the singer enters. Such examples are typical of the

composer's tendency to use heavier orchestration/tutti passages in the gaps the singer leaves: a conscious decision not to interfere with the singer.

35 George Steiner, *Errata: An Examined Life* (New Haven and London, 1997), p. 75.
36 Louis MacNeice, letter to T.S. Eliot, 22 November 1938, quoted in Robyn Marsack, *The Cave of Making: The Poetry of Louis MacNeice* (Oxford: Clarendon Press, 1982), p. 43. In the letter MacNeice refers to his *Autumn Journal*.
37 O'Siadhail's poetic record of this event is also found in 'Snow', *Our Double Time* (Newcastle upon Tyne: Bloodaxe Books, 1998), p. 31.
38 In 'Delivery' O'Siadhail varies the Wordsworthian sonnet with centrifugal rhyme (ABABCDCD EFGGFE); for O'Siadhail's handling of the sonnet form, see Kim Bridgford, 'In love with the World: O'Siadhail and the Sonnet' in *Musics of Belonging*, pp. 67-78.
39 See, for example, 'St Stephen's Green', *Our Double Time*, p. 123
40 James Joyce, *Ulysses* (London: Bodley, 1962), Chapter Two, pp. 67-69.
41 I refer here to the sharp decline of Latin following O'Malley's Free Education scheme of 1967; Declan Kiberd traces this in *The Irish Writer and the World* (Cambridge: Cambridge University Press, 2005), p. 275.
42 Flann O'Brien: *At Swim-Two-Birds* (London: Longmans, 1939), pp. 33-34. 'The College is outwardly a rectangular plain building with a fine porch where the midday sun pours down in summer from the Donnybrook direction, heating the steps for the comfort of the students. The hallway inside is composed of large black and white squares arranged in the orthodox chessboard pattern, and the surrounding walls, done in an unpretentious cream wash, bear three rough smudges caused by the heels, buttocks and shoulders of the students.'

Seóirse Bodley, The Naked Flame

Song Cycle for mezzo soprano (or baritone) and piano

Poetry: Michael O'Siadhail

Commissioned by RTÉ
(1987)

Each accidental applies to the note it prefixes and lasts for the rest of the bar at the same pitch

1. Tuning in

Micheal O'Siadhail

Seoirse Bodley

*All metronome markings in this cycle are intended as guidelines or approximations.

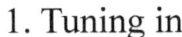

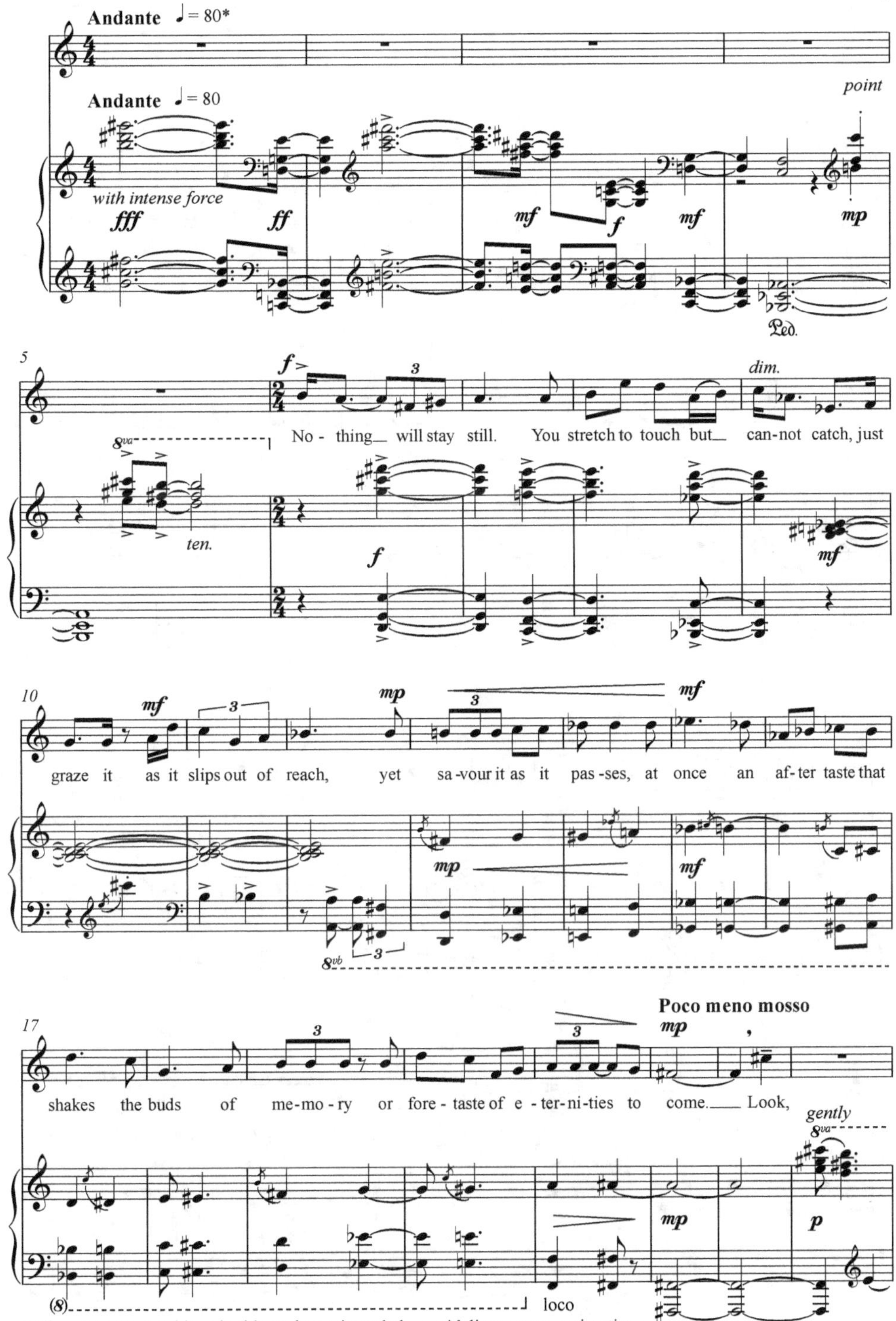

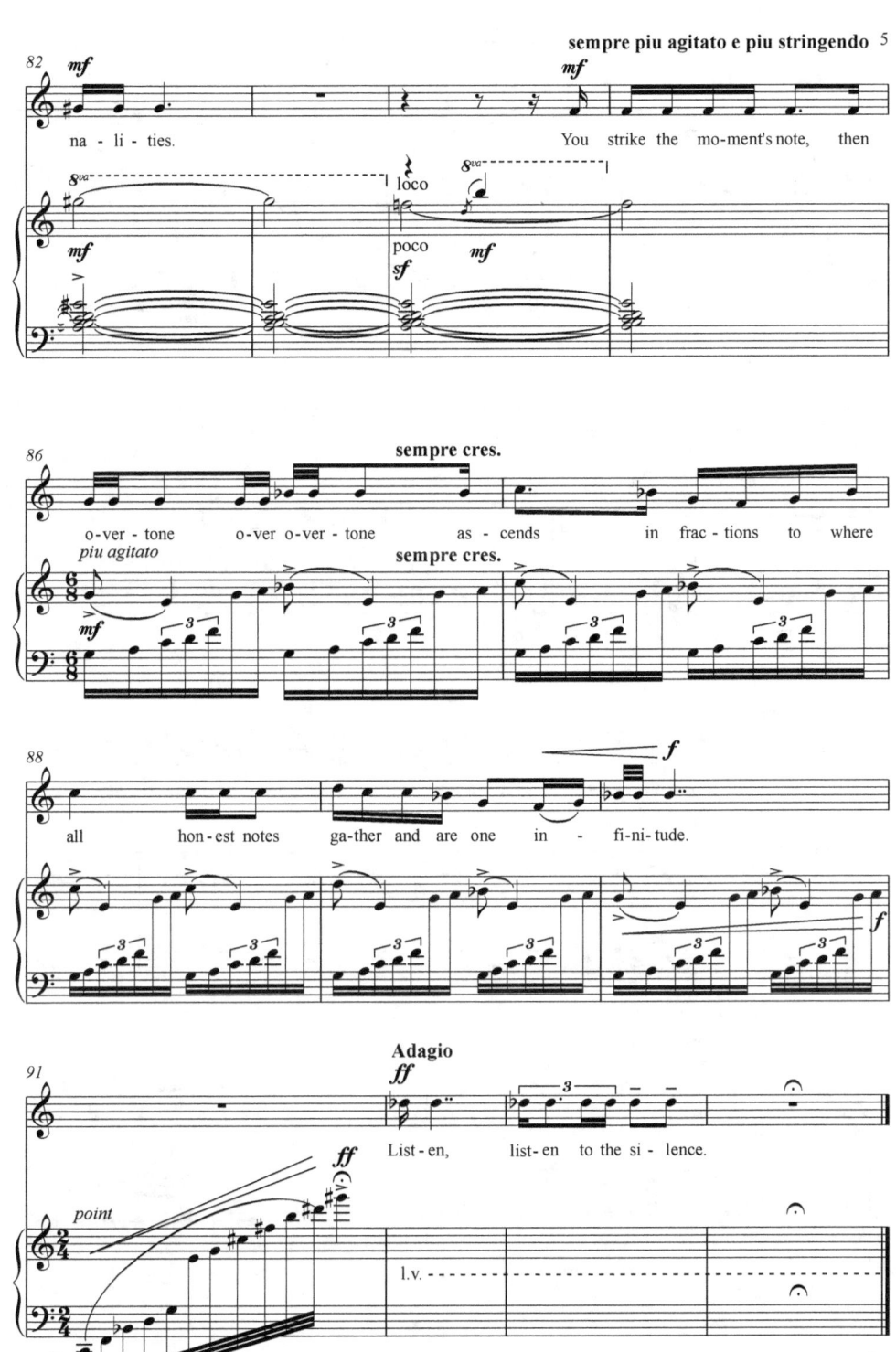

2. Rondo for Éamon

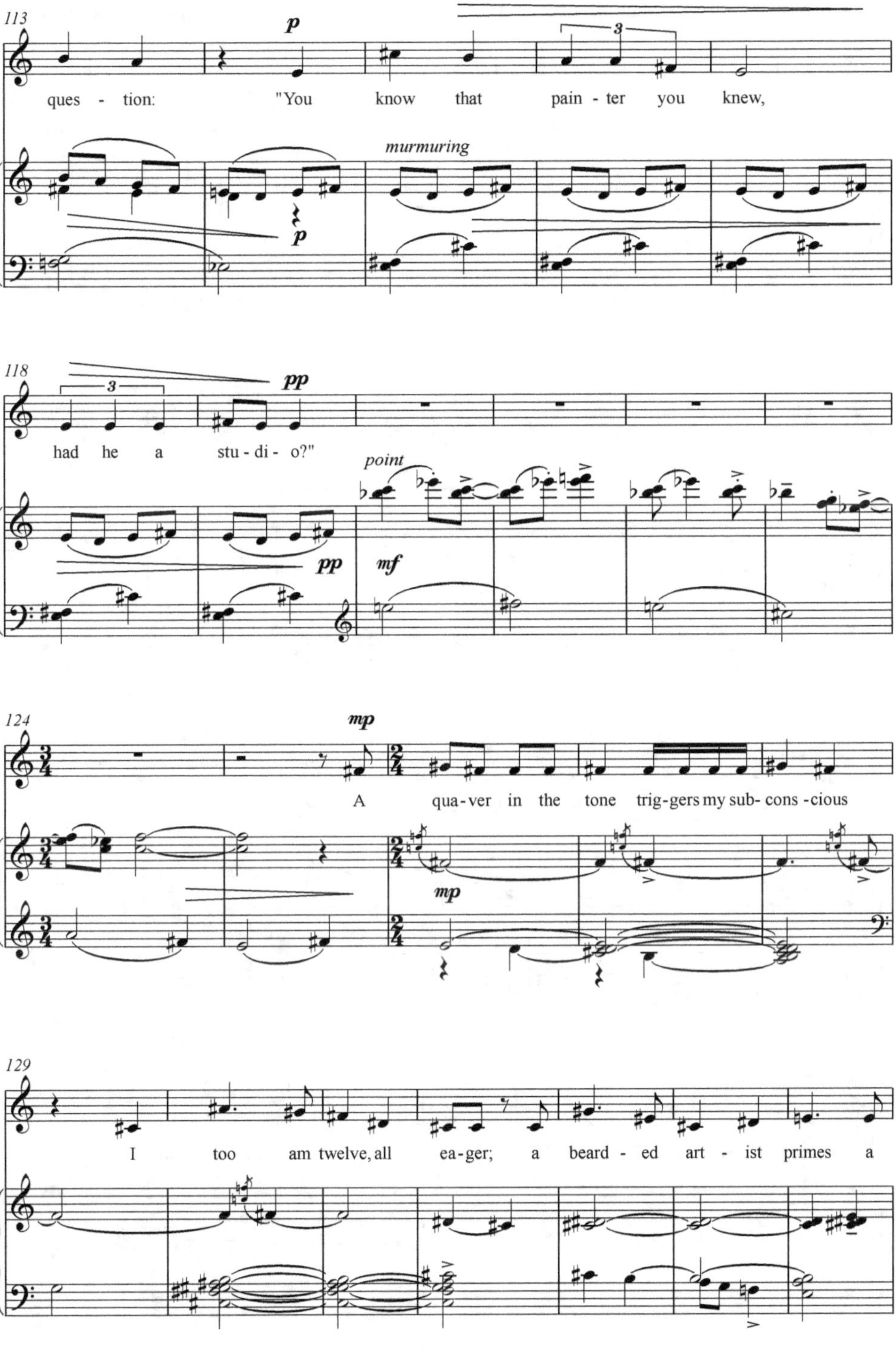
113
p
ques - tion: "You know that pain - ter you knew,
murmuring
p
118
pp
had he a stu - di - o?"
point
mf
pp
124
mp
A qua - ver in the tone trig - gers my sub - cons - cious
mp
129
I too am twelve, all ea - ger; a beard - ed art - ist primes a

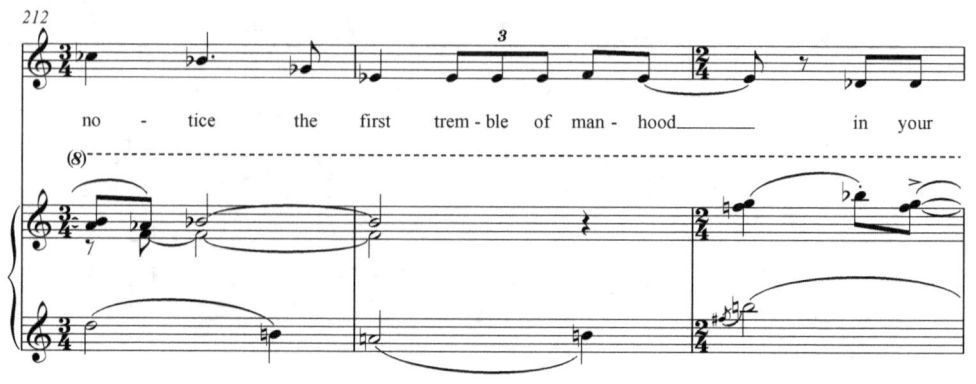
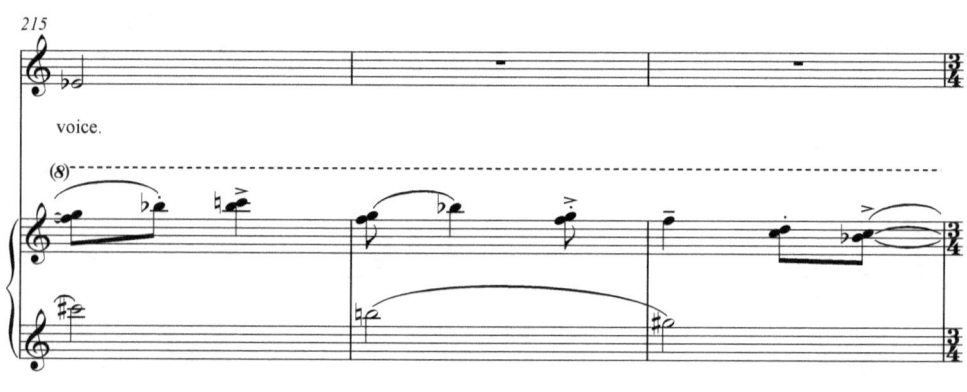
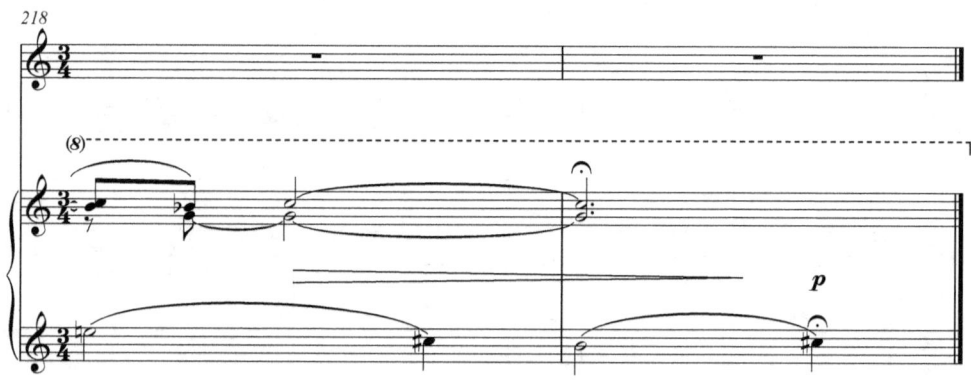

3. Those we follow

16

4. A Toast on the Eve

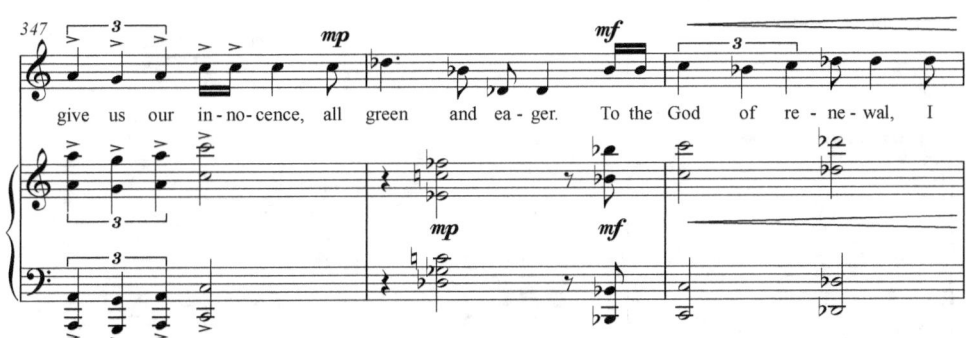
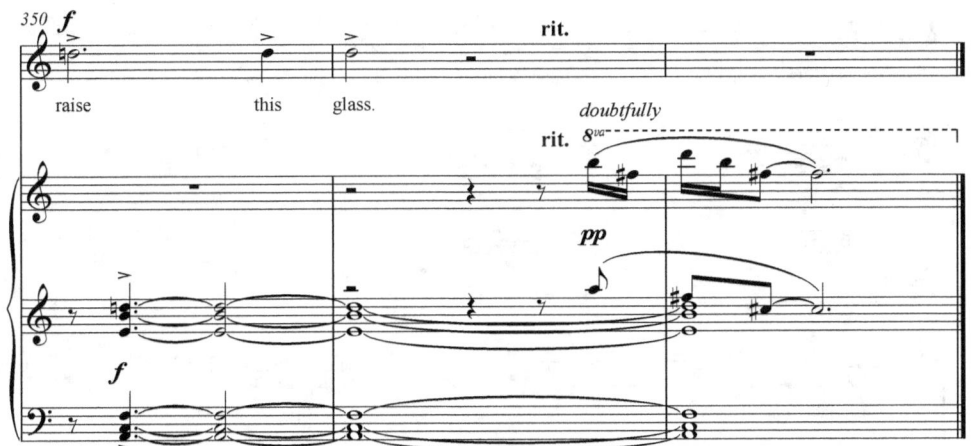

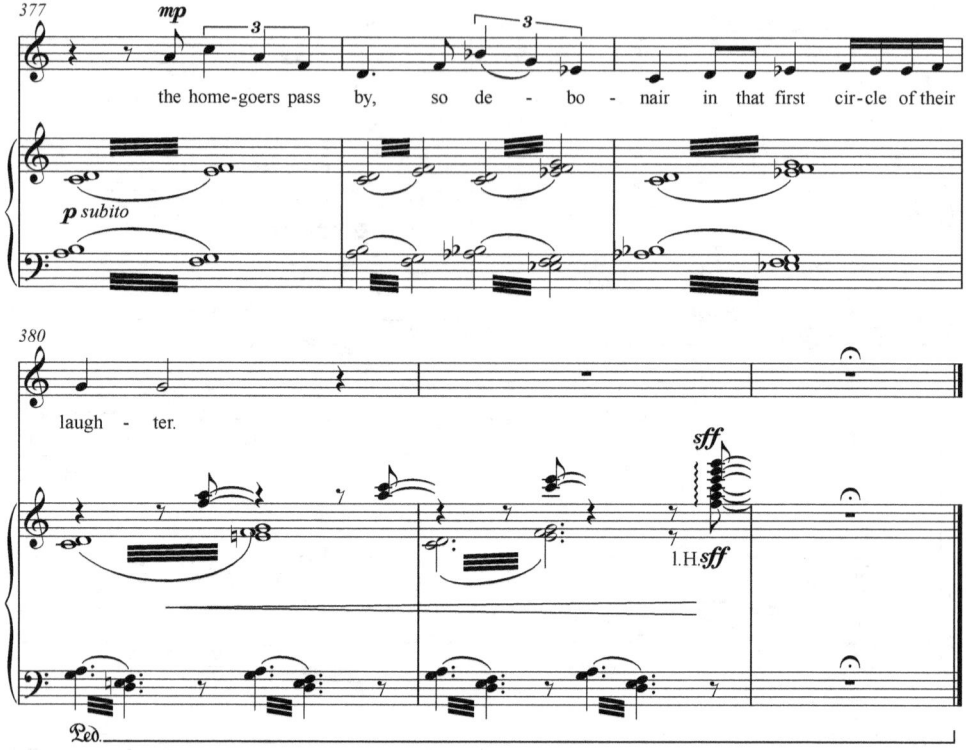

6. Hurt

7. Return

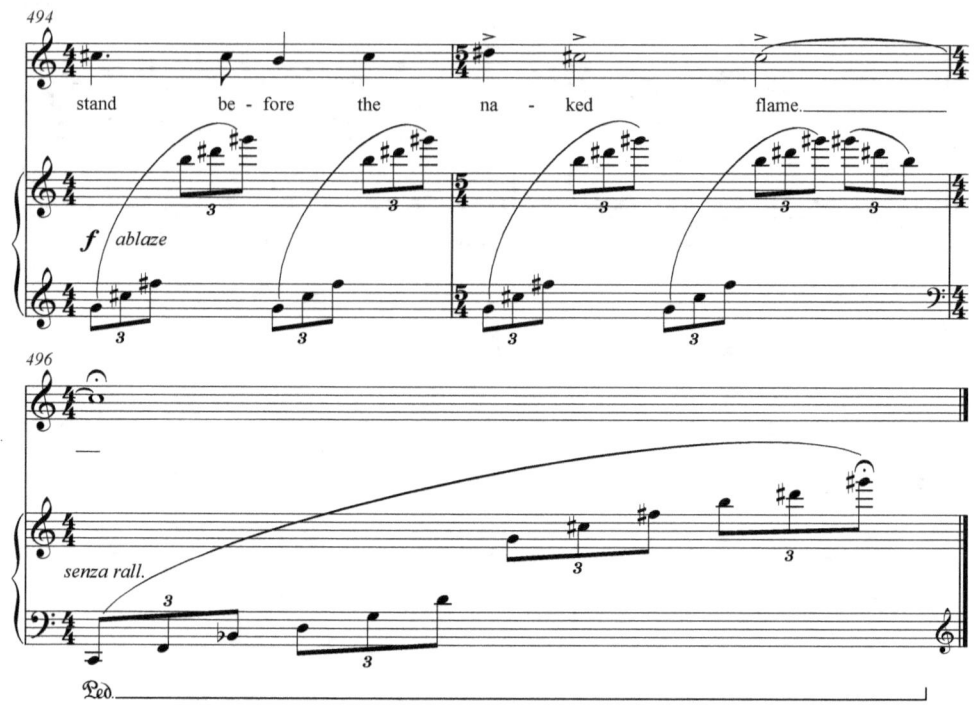

8. Love-song

*The rubato applies mainly to the *quasi parlando* repeated notes; the tempo should be slowed to accommodate the extra notes. There should be a seamless switch between singing & *quasi parlando*.

9. A Closure

10. Initiation

11. Hovering

*The spread of the chords is much slower here than at the opening of this song.

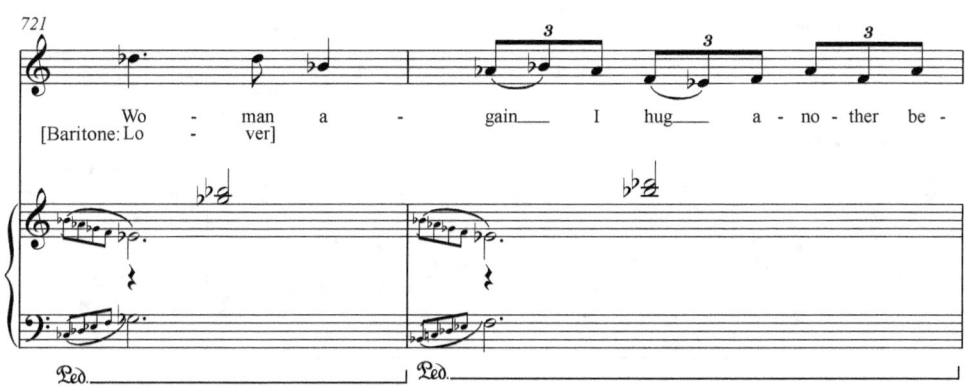
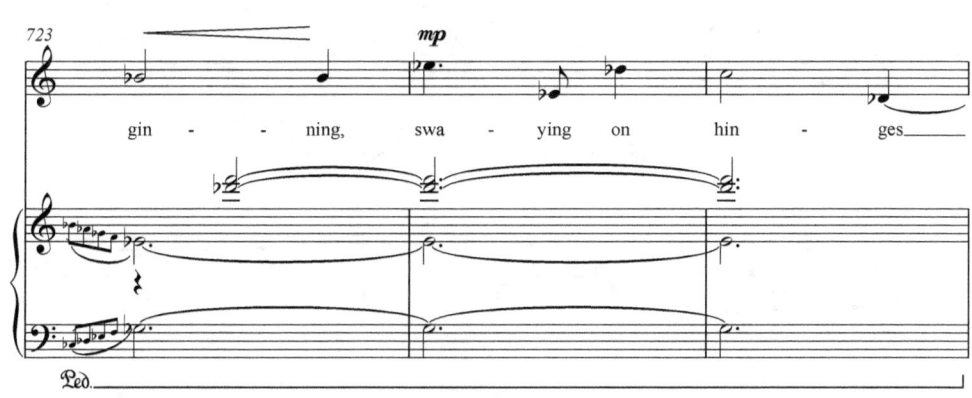

12. Rhapsody

Dublin 15-12-1987
Seóirse Bodley

Seóirse Bodley, Earlsfort Suite

Song Cycle for mezzo soprano (or baritone) and piano

Poetry: Michael O'Siadhail

Commissioned by Dúchas, The Heritage Service
(2000)

Each accidental applies to the note it prefixes and lasts for the rest of the bar at the same pitch

1. Delivery

Micheal O'Siadhail   **Seóirse Bodley**

2. Rite of Passage

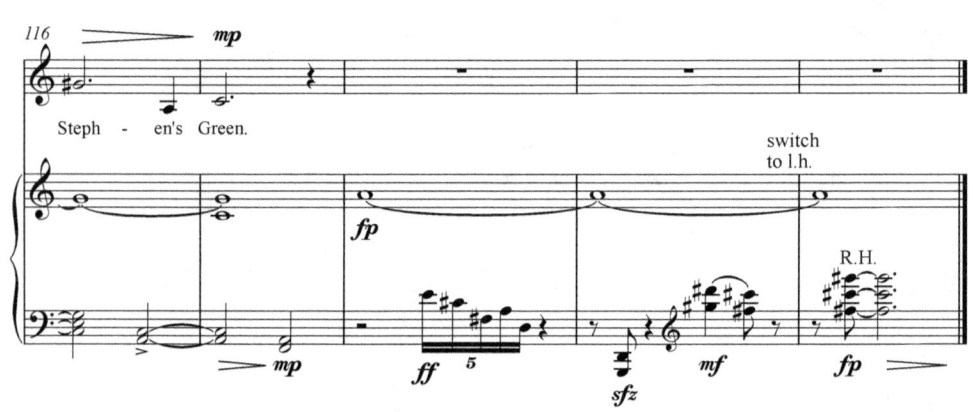

3. Streetscape

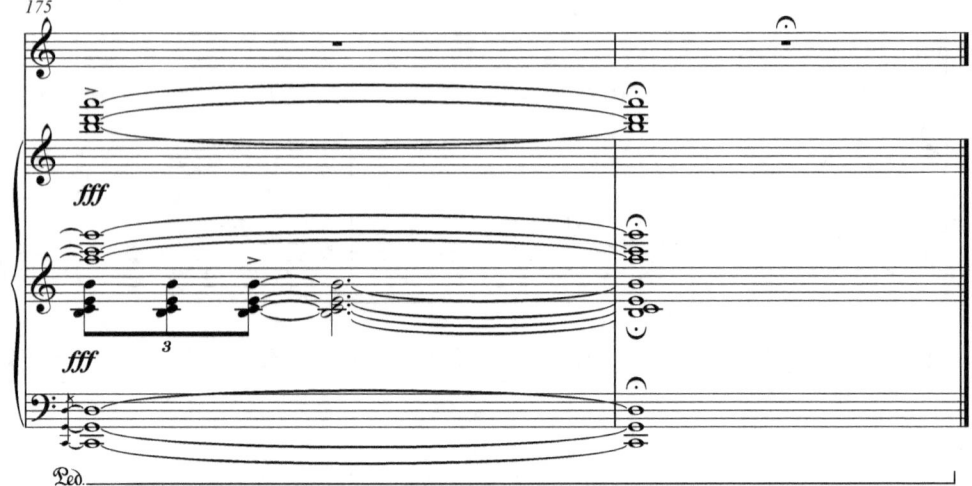

Appendix 1:

The Naked Flame

THE NAKED FLAME   Micheal O'Siadhail

1. Tuning In
Nothing will stay still. You stretch to touch
but cannot catch, just graze it as it slips
out of reach, yet savour it as it passes,
at once an aftertaste that shakes the buds
of memory or foretaste of eternities to come.
Look, there is the marvel! But as you look,
you look behind, beside, between, beyond.
The lush sumac hides crimson and banana
hues, fragrances remind both of bygones
and tomorrow, in the crow's foot and furrow
dimpled children smile, genes bloom,
eons glide between your butter-fingers –
have you so outgrown the age of time?
Prod of insight or knock on sanity's wall?
Scorch of wisdom's love or lure of madness!
A little quietude you ask, yet not
the balance that finds a point of equilibrium.

Rather choose the tense delight that knows
tug of was, pull of will-be, that is
the calm of motion you desire. Always
all hovers in its changing, every instant's
gene pivots possibilities, midpoints,
diminished chords that poise between tonalities.
You strike the moment's note, then overtone
over overtone ascends in fractions to where
all honest notes gather and are one
infinitude. Listen, listen to the silence!

2. Rondo For Eamon
Again that gangly earnestness.
'Actually, here's another I drew'
as I admire, dreamily a question;
'You know that painter you knew,

'had he a studio?' a quaver
in the tone triggers my subconscious;
I too am twelve, all eager;
a bearded artist primes a canvas.

I watch, gauche with enquiry.
'o no!', he said, 'my father
disapproved but when he died
I found my notices neatly folded

in his wallet, the good words
circled in red' – a posthumous
boost filling those voids,
years of unworded praise.

'Where was his studio!' A rondo;
now it's my turn to respond,
conscious that each syllable
may float a seed in the wind;

'on the seafront, so he saw
each morning a northern headland,
for years just kept drawing
that line in every weather'.

Is this the thrill of lineage!
I grow young in your ardour;
then crossing too soon your bridges,
fear those agonies in the garden.

You nod, frowning a little;
lightly the talk changes course.
I pretend not to notice the first
tremble of manhood in your voice.

3. Those we Follow

The best said little, yet enough to signal praise;
the best said least, never laid too heavy a hand;
just a glance of light, a path I might find,
but I followed false signs, stumbled into byways.

At last I retrace, begin the haul again –
the double-back that probes the double faith of loss
before gain. And then a patient glow of progress.
I so wanted them to know, to call to them:

O look what I have done! But they have gone
beyond the bend and out of sight.
I sway an instant, peering ahead; a voice resonates:
steady as you go, you carry someone's beacon.

4. A Toast on the Eve

Where is the star that winks in the east?
In this the nadir of the year, we sense
the drag of time. For a while deceased
friends trouble us – a glum roundabout
of memory. o beg a freshborn innocence,
some star to blink beyond a doubt.

Where is the star that signals in the east!
Tonight I am both adult and child;
I shape and plan and still am an unleased
tenant of my clay, never mistress of my history.
Ambitious and humble, I am reconciled
to bear this double witness to a mystery.

Where is the star that beckons to the east,
that God come down to bless the flesh

of living? O give us the daily yeast
to burble through the veins and charm
our sour grapes into wine. Find me the creche
where a God is cradled by woman's arm.

Where is the star that dances in the east?
Son of Ghost and Virgin forgive our meagre
welcome. Busy in the inns we feast
your arrival cribbed between the ox and ass.
O give us our innocence, all green and eager.
To the God of renewal, I raise this glass.

5. Debonair
Against a tide of yawning suburbanites,
up the morning's street a homing débutante
links her dinner-jacketed cavalier, last night's
fling a carnation raffish in her ebony hair.

A waking flower opens to her story's theme
unfolding in amazement timeless journeys of renewal;
close-packed petals widening the rings of her dream.

A downstreet commuter, out of the tail of my eye
I catch her recklessness, the panache of such a beginning;
a rip-tide of energy, the home-goers pass by,
so debonair in that first circle of their laughter.

6. Hurt
Your music took me by surprise; nothing
by halves, I matched you move for move,
I warmed, I opened, I yielded, I loved.
You of all people to double cross!

Is it anger that stings or is it shame?
Intimacy cuts both ways: I've mapped
your nakedness: do I pay you back
(that way you'd have called the tune)

or withdraw, wear an aggrieved look,
sullen air of those who finding the world
guilty, seal off all the risks, turn
a deaf ear to buffeting moods and rhythms?

Against the beat, between the throbs,
our moments leap and fall, jazz
notes of ecstasy, random arabesques
of anguish. a hazardous melody of being.

I reel with pain, half anger, half shame;
reckless, over again, I gave everything,
Twice shy, I know I must curb the swing,
I know that I must watch my step.

But I know that I know nothing.
All that is certain is change. I plan
to gauge every footfall, but in the dance
my steps grow wide-hipped and lavish.

7. Return

The finesse of re-beginnings! Here like a novice
I seem to thrill at every spendthrift word
as we dispense ourselves in flares of newness.

We angle between the coyness of once intimates,
stiffness of half-strangers and allow our dead
image of each other quicken and become.

There have been so many dreams and stumbles,
infinitesimal shifts, inches of slow growth,
impalpable moves to make the same so different.

I hankered after you. Despite our separate
ways, our trade in coolness, something of the flame
abides, sputters between desire and memory.

I confess my need to trim the blurred wick,
I love the thrift of shared ground, returns
to older trust, subtle closures of rift.

Hurt, jealousies, misunderstanding or drift?
Let's say it was a silence where we hoarded
the sealed years of business we now swap.

Wait! Supposing, how can we now be sure?
I shy from fire. You insist I drop veil
after veil; we stand before the naked flame.

8. Love-Song

In early spring, talk still young and highflown,
we laughed, there was an endless time to flirt
and toy with the fable of a year. A snowdrop afloat
in an old wineglass on our table, already grown
tumid with water, lifted the panels of her skirt
to show the pale green hem of her petticoat.

Soon we are strolling along the edge of a bay
kicking over the smudged traces of an early swimmer.
It's deep into June; summer lush and unplanned
rocks us in its lazy arms. In the blaze of day
we paddle in the shallows; I watch as through a shimmer
of water the sun doodles honeycombs in the sand.

A year tilts into autumn; after its madcap
race the Russian vine issues its manifesto,
a spray of flower; the sun sloping in humility

smiles its frail approval as old men wrap
against the chill. At last I think I know
half of what we love is love's fragility.

On a winter evening as I turn into our street,
I hurry to see the rim of light that fingers
around the curtain's edge to tell you're home.
You open the door and I sense as we meet
our moment's wonder. A scent lingers;
I breathe deeply to feed my memory's honeycomb.

9. A Closure
Only why, why should you've left,
broken our promise of forever?
Though the mind relives your end –
captive in the lurch, my heart rebels.

I've drawn the brittle circle full:
finder, keeper, loser, weeper;
some guilt still bickers,
listing old unseized chances. But no,

I won't mourn. Why should I?
We gave our gifts – there's nothing
to wish undone. Nothing and everything –
what do I do with all this love?

So lightly you'd quipped: and if I quit
first, I hope you find whoever
waits for you – surely our spirits
could manage such a ménage à trois!

Where are you, lover! At the whim
of every breeze, every breaker,
I'm pitched starboard or port,
my boat of moods lunges forward.

Then, just dallying alone, drifting
in our spaces, former common haunts,
shared moorings of delight, I calm,
touching down where we'd been together.

I grieve for you, I need to grope
my maze of anguish, to work the dark
slowly. I'll ripen in my sorrow,
I'll search for you in every face.

10. Initiation (for Seamus)
Box, cut, deal: I retrieve
neglected words, squibs of recollection,
wet afternoons of beggar-my-neighbour.

'Deuces', I explain, 'juices!' you laugh,

toying with ambiguity. Every term
detonates magic or flush of memory.

Caught in your playfulness I breathe
forgotten excitements, dead-pan
turn of card, flutter before showdown.

Still too conscious of burnt fingers –
'hold those cards close to your chest!'
Am I too anxious to teach guile?

Bids, tricks, bluff beyond you,
all moods flit across your eye.
Should you not keep such innocence?

In your growth I grow; at one
remove, reshuffle my first fumblings:
your road out, my road back.

11. Hovering
Watch those eyes deepen hue.
A world outside loses its grip;
I drown in his glance –
can this be me?

Surely that was an age ago –
Ablush, skittish as a young girl,
my being expands, that look envelops me.

But more and differently: inward spoors,
trials of womanhood cut channels
along the years nearer to the source.

I dare what I never dared then.
Still I hover like a fledgling,
need to hold
this rapture in focus.

I relearn doubts and jealousy, a débutante
craving the fitful ebbs and flows
of sweet madness,
of first ecstasy.

Then the dream grows and grows.
Woman again I hug another beginning,
swaying on hinges of our everyday.

12. Rhapsody
This love that is forever is in motion,
a coiling stream of now and now and now.
Remember, you say, remember a wistful time,
a sunlit age, upstream once and long ago,
a paradise of past when all was well –

how things have changed! Or tomorrow you say,
tomorrow, maybe downstream soon and hilly
in the green far-away, if only when,
if only then you say – but it is now
a world of happening forever is in motion,
now and here nothing will stand still,
our point of departure the actual: though
we search for footholds in what was or will be
or with a god's eye view attempt detachment
to minimize our risks, human and fallible we
trust the love that is surrender to the flow.
In all this flux perhaps some patterns form;
eddies, rondos of experience, spirals, spheres
of remembrance, loops of history, forecast or guess;
yet you are never there, never have arrived
for there is no status quo, moment by moment
like planets tense within our orbits we trust,
we choose, we act and so become our story,
we do and tell our own once upon a time.
Still there is room for surprise; we live
at the mercy of each new event, beck
and call of mystery, vulnerable to how it is.
Speak of glancing water or ever-fresh
configurations of a sky; flowing and mutable,
this love that is forever is in motion
and every here and now a widening ring.

Appendix 2:

Earlsfort Suite

EARLSFORT SUITE   Micheal O'Siadhail

1. Delivery
This is my street. Here I come wandering in.
The Stella Maris Home: a stone's throw
From a park entrance where bronze Fates spin,
As Nineteen-Forty-Seven is gathering snow.
A Bedouin boy stumbles on Dead Sea Scrolls;
The year of carbon-dating and Hekla's fire,
Of 'New Look' hem-lines and platform soles,
Prokofiev's Sixth, A Streetcar Named Desire.
Maybe I can't and still I fancy I recall
Just a busy pavement at the corner of a town
Where a woman tucks me in the mood and tone
Of a year that sinks and carbons into my bone
As a lava of pure desire comes scrolling down
And skies of January snow begin to fall.

2. Rite of Passage
Nervous last minute tips, high-strung recall
Of swotted months as we crossed
A foyer's chessboard floor to the Exam Hall

Where an attendant lays out a paper in Latin
As a fervid concentration descends,
A tuned-in orchestra hushed under the baton.

All my life as soon as I begin to tense or fret
Same maze of a nightmare:
Again this June afternoon where I sweat

Against the clock through a passage of unseen
To follow the thread of a clue
Back to my Fates at a corner of Stephen's Green.

3. Streetscape
A street in which our days and bricks conspire
And walls have ears to hear and make their own
Whole symphonies of remembrance and desire.

Stella Maris vanished as a city began to grow
And boom but still on this honking boulevard
Pillars of what was our exam chamber's portico

That now canopy the doors to a concert hall's
Vestibule. As listeners hush to the raised baton
A silence of nervous memory echoes in its walls.

Lives cast in the light and tenor of a streetscape
That gathers up our musics in stick and stone.
Our shells and selves shaped by what we shape.

www.ingramcontent.com/pod-product-compliance
Lightning Source LLC
Chambersburg PA
CBHW070739230426
43669CB00014B/2508